YESHUA,
SON OF MAN

YESHUA,
SON OF MAN

CHERIAN MATHEWS

PARTRIDGE
A Penguin Random House Company

To order additional copies of this book, contact
Partridge India
000 800 10062 62
orders.india@partridgepublishing.com

www.partridgepublishing.com/india

PREFACE

This book is a novel - a work of fiction. As the title indicates, it is about Yeshua, which is the Hebrew version of the name Jesus. But unlike the Jesus whom Christians worship, Yeshua, Son of Man, is not divine, but just a human being. The purpose of the book is to figure out how a wholly human Yeshua could have lived and carried out his mission, and how the world would have received him.

Jesus is distinguished by his teachings which reveal his enormous knowledge. If we accept that Jesus is Son of God, it is easy to explain his knowledge and wisdom - he inherited it from God, his father. However, if he was only son of man, then one wonders how he got his knowledge and wisdom. Obviously his parents could not afford any costly schooling for their son. His education is not mentioned in the gospels, or anywhere else in the Bible. In fact, there is no information given in the gospels about his life from the age of twelve to thirty. What he did and where he went during this period have great relevance to subsequent events.

The author imagines that Yeshua, Son of Man, got his knowledge and wisdom through education and hard work. He studied the Jewish scriptures in Jerusalem, where he toiled hard to master not only Tanaka but also languages such as Hebrew, Aramaic and Greek. It is through painstaking effort that he studied manuscripts available to him in Hebrew—both old and new. He did not have to pay for this, as it came as the reward for his thirst for knowledge and his performance.

After learning all he could in Jerusalem, Yeshua travelled in a trade caravan to Taxila University in the East to study Buddhism and Hinduism, which were the prevailing religions there at that time. As he had no scholarship to start with, he taught Aramaic to traders to meet his expenses. Since the language of instruction at the University was Pali, he had to become proficient in this new language. This he learnt as a part time student in the School of Languages, with the help of the Acharya's (Dean's) daughter, Shakuntala. When he won the King's scholarship, which paid for his tuition and boarding, he was enrolled in the School of Religion to study Buddhism under the guidance of Acharya Shantideva. Yeshua not only learned Buddhism, but also practiced it. He did not forget to make himself familiar with the Ayurvedic system of medicine. On graduating with high honours, the Acharya suggested the he lead a course on Comparative Religion. Yeshua, who was responsible for the whole course, was expected to teach Judaism, while Shakuntala, the pretty and accomplished daughter of Acharya Sahadeva, was asked to teach a course in Hinduism. This course turned out to be an outstanding success, both because of the content and presentation, but also because of the open discussions which were encouraged by the teachers. Yeshua and Shakuntala, who had become good friends from the time she helped him learn Pali, became very close to each other during the joint course they conducted. Shakuntala also helped him to learn Sanskrit, the language in which the Hindu Scriptures were composed. Their association took a romantic turn, with Shakuntala suggesting that Yeshua should settle down in Taxila and marry her. Yeshua told her about his dream of a Mission to the Jews, which he had cherished for a long time. Shakuntala persuaded him to go on a picnic on Margala hills, during which they became quite intimate. Yeshua promised her that if her ever married, she would be his bride, but his mission was his first priority.

As Yeshua was pondering over the events of the previous ten years sitting in his room, an earth quake struck Taxila. The capital Sirkap and the School of Languages, housed in buildings made of stone blocks, were the worst hit. It took the lives of King Gondophares, and Acharya Sahadeva. Yeshua stayed on to help Shakuntala to cremate her father and to start life anew.

In the course of ten years that he spent in Taxila, Yeshua evolved a theology that combined the best in the three major religions of that time. After absorbing all this knowledge, he left everything and went back to his native land on a mission of teaching and reinterpreting the Scripture to the Jews. For over three years he preached to crowds of people, who gathered in large numbers to hear him speak, in parables, about human problems and the Kingdom of God. Righteousness was the key word he used to describe this Kingdom. He argued that the rigid Jewish laws should be enforced with compassion. He also conducted a healing mission, in which Ayurveda played a key role. Finally he went to the Temple in Jerusalem on a cleansing mission. The priests got worried about this threat to their very existence and managed to get him crucified. However, with the help of his friends and supporters, he escaped from the gallows.

After escaping from the cross, Yeshua appeared before his disciples a few times, but realised that they were thinking that he was the 'risen' Yeshua. He got reliable information that the Jewish hierarchy was looking for him. Recognising the threat to his life, as he was already pronounced dead on the cross by a Roman Centurion, Yeshua managed to reach Edessa which was a small but independent State in which neither the Jews nor the Romans had any influence. From Edessa he returned to Taxila University, where a faculty position was waiting for him. He also married the girl who was patiently waiting for him all this time. Acharya Shantideva, who was keeping in touch with events in Palestine, explained to Yeshua that a young scholar in Jewish scriptures named Paul had built a Church based on Yeshua's life and teachings, but portraying him as the Son of God who went back to heaven. His message appealed to the Greek population that lived on the rim of the Mediterranean Sea.

CHAPTER 1

Scripture Studies in Jerusalem

Yeshua looked at the shimmering waters of the Sea of Galilee. Though this sight was quite familiar, it always had a mesmerising effect on him. This fresh water lake was wrongly called a sea because of its size: 21 km long and 13 km wide. It was early morning and the sun was shining bright. A gentle breeze blowing from the sea caressed his face leaving a nice, cool feeling. The place was already bustling with activity. Fishing boats were on the job, taking advantage of the favourable weather conditions in the morning, as against the evening when the Sea of Galilee was known for stormy weather and high winds. Yeshua was a frequent visitor to the small patch of sandy beach on the south western coast of the Sea. Today he had a companion, who was also looking intently at the fishing boats. Yohan was his cousin brother, just about six months older than him, who had come down from Jerusalem for his Bar Mitzvah.

Bar Mitzvah is a ceremony that every Jewish boy had to undergo when he reached the age of thirteen. It represented the coming of age of a Jew. Yeshua's Bar Mitzvah was a special occasion for his family, not only because he was the first born son of Yosef and Miriam, but also because he was better educated in Jewish Scriptures than his contemporaries. Yeshua recalled in his mind the events of the previous day with pleasure. Yohan, his cousin and friend, had come for this function and that was how they could spend some time together on the shore of the Sea of Galilee early next morning. Yohan knew that Yosef and Miriam were ordinary people who lived in a modest dwelling where a private conversation was not possible. Nor could they afford an expensive education for their son. After all Yosef was only a carpenter. So Yohan asked Yeshua directly: "How did you get admission in Gamaliel's Academy? I have heard that it is very difficult to be selected for that course".

Yeshua replied: "You may remember that I went to the Temple with my parents a year ago. While they were busy with the sacrifice that they wanted to perform, I wandered around the place, and got into a room full of bearded people who looked like the Rabbi whose classes I attended in Nazareth. I told them that I had some questions about the Scriptures. A bearded man who looked like the High Priest exclaimed: "what impertinence! Call the guards and throw him out". Another bearded man, whom I later identified as Rabbi Gamaliel, intervened saying that he would talk to me and find out what my questions were. *Sometimes good questions come from youngsters,* he told the High Priest."

Rabbi Gamaliel gestured to Yeshua to wait outside. He came out after sometime and asked the lad what his questions were. Yeshua had two questions.

1. Why is YAHWEH a jealous God, as stated in the Scriptures? If he is the one true God, who is he jealous of?
2. Why was Adam and Eve sent out of the Garden of Eden? If God did not want them to eat the fruit of the Tree of Knowledge, he could have planted that tree elsewhere. It appears to me that they were trapped.

"Gamaliel wanted to know whether I had asked these questions to my teacher back in my hometown. I said that indeed I had asked these questions, but I was told not to ask such questions. Gamaliel then asked me my age and, on being told that I was 12 years old, he said: *You are an intelligent youngster who needs more education. Anyway, it is time you started your Bar Mitzvah training. Come and join my Scripture Academy, when I give the next training. There we can discuss all your questions. But first a priest must certify that you are twelve years old and that at least one of your parents is a Levite.* "That is no problem", I said: "Priest Zachariah is my uncle. I will request him to give the certificate. The problem is that my father Yosef cannot afford to pay the fees". The Rabbi had his answer: *Fees, I will waive for a bright boy like you. I will speak to a rich man who supports such causes. Meet me tomorrow with the certificate from Priest Zachariah."*

Yohan: "Then what happened?"

Yeshua: "Just then my parents approached us asking: *where have you disappeared, Yeshua? We were looking for you all over the place.* It was Rabbi Gamaliel who answered that question, saying: *We are discussing the Scripture,* and he walked away. "Isn't that Gamaliel?" asked Father and Mother at the same time. I narrated the whole conversation to them and suggested a visit to Priest Zachariah's house. Mother enthusiastically agreed. The reception that my mother got from Aunt Elisabeth showed me that the two cousin sisters were very close to each other. Priest Zachariah, your father, was happy to give the certificate, stating that one of the parents was a Levite. He told me that he was happy that at least one boy from the family had shown interest in studying the Scripture, perhaps implying that his own son was not so interested in pursuing his father's profession".

Yohan responded: "That is exactly what I expected him to say. He does not know that I am also studying the Scripture, but elsewhere." Yeshua wanted to find out where Yohan was studying, but seeing his cousin in an angry mood, he kept quiet.

Yosef and Miriam was an average couple living in a small town called Nazareth, which was within an hour's walk from the Sea of Galilee. Though they lived in Nazareth, Yeshua had heard it said that he was born in Bethlehem, as his parents had to travel to Jerusalem at the time of his birth to register in the census ordered by the Caesar and conducted by King Herod. Herod died over a year after the census. Though he was referred to as Herod the Great, most people did not credit him with that title, especially the Jews. He was a brutal King (actually the client King of Romans) who murdered his father-in-law, several of his ten wives and his two elder sons. He taxed his people heavily for his construction projects. What is more, he was not a Jew, but an Edumian. When Herod died, he had left a Will dividing his kingdom among his three surviving sons. According to this, Archelaus the senior most got half the kingdom in the form of Judea proper, Philip II got Gualanitis, and Antipas got Galilee and Perea. While approving the will, Emperor Octavian gave them the titles of Ethnarch to Archelaus, and Tetrarch (ruler of a quarter) for the other two. Later the Emperor dismissed Archelaus from his post for inefficiency and combined Judea and Samaria into a prefecture under a prefect named Valerius Gratus.

It was the thirteenth year of the reign of Herod Antipas, the tetrarch of Galilee and Perea when Yeshua had his Bar Mitzvah. Antipas had a better rapport with his subjects than his father, as he gave religious freedom to the predominantly Jewish population. However, the Pharisees and the Sadducees did not like him because he broke the Law by marrying Herodias, who was the divorced wife of his brother Herod Philip I. For this purpose he had divorced his first wife and incurred the wrath of his father-in-law, King Aretas IV of Nabatea, which was just east of Perea.

Yeshua enjoyed his studies in Gamaliel's Academy. He worked hard and earned the appreciation of Gamaliel because he gained expertise in Torah. Gamaliel took particular care in teaching Hebrew, emphasising reading and writing skills. Yeshua reserved his basic questions to a later date after Bar Mitzvah. Gamaliel accepted his proposal to celebrate his Bar Mitzvah in his native town of Nazareth, on the condition that he would go back to the Scripture Academy to complete the three year course. Yosef and Miriam were happy to organise their son's Bar Mitzvah party to which they invited their neighbours and relatives. On the appointed day, the whole family went to the synagogue and Yeshua read the assigned portion of the Torah with ease and grace. He also gave an interpretation of the passage that he read. After the service, everyone congratulated the proud parents, and Miriam glowed in the praise. Later there was a lunch at Yosef's residence, specially cooked by Miriam. Yeshua received many presents from the guests. After all the guests left, the parents sat with Yeshua to discuss his future plans. Yosef asked his son: "When would you like to start as an apprentice?" "Gamaliel has asked me to continue this course in the Scriptures. It is a rigorous course which is of three years' duration", replied the son. "So you have decided to be a priest? That is better than becoming a carpenter", said Miriam. "Let me first finish the course; then we will think about priesthood", said Yeshua. "How often can you come home, once you join this course", wondered the mother. "Mother, it is a three year course. I understand that a short break is given at the end of each year", was the reply. "It must be rather expensive; how will we pay for it?" Yosef asked with concern. "You don't have to worry about the cost, Father; It is all arranged by the Rabbi." assured Yeshua. "You must have impressed the Rabbi with your performance", exclaimed the proud mother.

When Yeshua passed the three year course with distinction, Gamaliel suggested that he join the advanced course. This advanced course was generally meant for those preparing for priesthood. Yeshua signed up for two reasons: [1] he was interested in learning the scriptures and [2] this was the best education he could get without paying any fees. The expenses were underwritten by rich Jews and the admission was at the sole discretion of Rabbi Gamaliel. The advanced course was indeed quite rigorous. The Rabbi insisted on language skills. Most of his students could speak Hebrew and Aramaic, but lacked reading and writing skills. Yeshua had already acquired these skills in the first course itself and could help the Rabbi in training his fellow students. Old Hebrew was needed to read old manuscripts in the library. Greek was the contemporary language, which was useful in interacting with the Government Officials. Latin was also included in the syllabus because the rulers were Romans. Yeshua excelled in languages and spent long hours in going through old manuscripts, which was easy because he was put in charge of the library. Gamaliel taught Tanaka from the beginning to the end, using both written and oral versions as well as his own interpretations. In reading the text of consonants of Old Hebrew with some applied vowel alphabets, vocalisation was very important. Yeshua practiced the oral rendering to the full satisfaction of the Rabbi.

Yeshua learned that Tanaka consisted of 24 books in three parts. 5 books of Torah (Genesis, Exodus, Leviticus, Numbers, and Deuteronomy) constituted the first part. Part two was Nevi'im or Prophets, which consisted of Joshua, Judges, Samuel I & II, Kings I & II, Isaiah, Jeremiah, Ezekiel and twelve minor prophets, namely, Hosea, Joel, Amos, Obadiah, Jonah, Micah, Nahum, Habakkuk, Zephaniah, Haggai, Zechariah, and Malachi. Since the last group was counted as one book, the total count of books reached only 13 at this stage. Part III was Ketuvim or Writings. This consisted of 11 books - Psalms, Proverbs, Job, Song of Songs, Ruth, Lamentations, Ecclesiastes, Esther, Daniel, Ezra-Nehemiah, and Chronicles (I & II), thus taking the total count to 24.

In order to make the course interesting, Gamaliel first cited human-interest stories, and then brought out how YHWH [to be pronounced as YAHWEH or YAHOWAH depending on the vowels you insert] was behind the whole of history. He laid special emphasis on the Law of Moses and explained how this was elaborated by later Rabbis to take into account various human situations. The entire history of Israel could be explained by the sequence: disobedience, punishment and repentance. The prophets of Israel played an important role in guiding the nation back to repentance from their sinful ways. Yeshua found the classes on Ketuvim enjoyable, in particular Psalms which were sung by the whole class during chant sessions. After completing the advanced course, Yeshua went home to his parents. When Yohan came to visit, the two cousins met again on the banks of the Sea of Galilee. Yeshua gave Yohan a brief account of the course he had completed, but his cousin was not quite satisfied.

"This is something that every Jew knows", said Yohan."Tell me what is different about Gamaliel's teaching?" "You have made a statement and then asked a question" answered Yeshua. "I will respond to them one by one. Every Jew does not know the entire Tanaka; at least I did not know until I went to Gamaliels's Academy. What I knew before that was only the Torah. Even the teacher in Nazareth did not teach the full Tanaka, though he knew about it and could tell us many interesting stories like that of Jonah spending three days and nights inside a fish. He also knew the names of some prophets like Isaiah and Jeremiah and the names of some of our kings. In particular, nobody had access to the scrolls containing the written version of Tanaka. On the other hand, I could study them for the first time during my course. The Prophesies become more meaningful when you read the text, than when you hear distorted stories. Psalms come alive when you read the verses rather than when you hear them as a ritual. We had chant sessions in which the whole class sang the psalms in unison. I particularly liked Psalm 127 of Solomon, which I will recite for you.

Unless the Lord builds the house,
The builders labor in vain.
Unless the Lord watches over the city,
The guards stand watch in vain.
In vain you rise early
and stay up late,
Toiling for food to eat—
For he grants sleep to those he loves.
Children are a heritage from the Lord,
Offspring a reward from him.
Like arrows in the hands of a warrior

Are children born in one's youth.
Blessed is the man
Whose quiver is full of them.
They will not be put to shame
When they contend with their opponents in court.

Coming to your question how the course was different, let me say that it was new and interesting. First of all, the Rabbi gave a lot of importance to languages. Because of that, I am comfortable with three languages – Hebrew, Aramaic and Greek. I can also converse in Latin. In fact, old Hebrew should be considered as another language, because its alphabet had no vowels. As far as Scripture is concerned, the difference is in his interpretations and commentary. This also gave us a lot of scope for discussion and questions. I could ask many doubts", replied Yeshua.

He continued: "Of special interest to me was the teaching of Jewish history from the beginning to the current time. We started with the story of creation, continued with the expulsion of Adam & Eve from the Garden of Eden for disobedience and went on to the Great Flood which destroyed every living being except Noah and his family along with a pair of each species that they carried with them in the Ark. Noah's family multiplied rapidly and became a threat even to God. So God introduced confusion among them by making them speak in different languages. Then YHWH selected Abraham to be the father of his chosen people. Abraham left his native place in Mesopotamia and moved to Canaan, His son Isaac succeeded him as the Patriarch of this new tribe of people. Isaac's son Jacob succeeded him and got the name Israel for himself and his people. The whole new nation of three generations now moved to Egypt to escape a famine. After a few generations they became slaves in Egypt. Now Moses arose as a great leader and led them out of Egypt. God made them wander around the desert for forty years. Moses died at the threshold of Canaan; so his trusted deputy Joshua took over the leadership. He conquered the southern region of Canaan and settled the tribes of Judah and Benjamin there. Though he divided up the rest of Canaan for the remaining tribes, he died before conquering and clearing the new territory. For the next many decades Israel was leaderless. They were subjugated by their enemies for part of the time, but periodically a leader arose when they repented and prayed to YAHWEH. These occasional leaders were known as Judges; some of them good, the others bad. Disgusted with this state of affairs, the people requested Prophet Samuel to plead with YAHWEH to give governance to a King. Accordingly Saul was anointed as King. He soon lost favour with YAHWEH who replaced him with David, who was a popular King. He was succeeded by Solomon who became the most famous of the Kings of Israel. After Solomon's death only two tribes stayed with his son, but the rest went with Jeroboam to form the northern kingdom. This kingdom ended about two and a half centuries later, when the Assyrian King conquered its capital Samaria and transported its people to other parts of the Empire. Judea, however, survived for another century. Babylonian King Nebuchadnezzar ransacked the Temple of Jerusalem, and took all the smart people as prisoners and marched them off to Babylon."

"Alright, alright" responded Yohan. "Perhaps I had access to more information than you had since I grew up in a priest's family. Now please tell me what your questions were and whether you got your answers".

Yeshua: "Well, you already know my first two questions. 1. Why is YHWH jealous? Who is he jealous of? 2. Why were Adam and Eve sent out of the Garden of Eden?

In fact, all my questions can be classified into two groups: 1. Nature and characteristics of YHWH and our Patriarchs, and 2. Authenticity of the Scripture.

I will now give examples of the first group. Since the first two questions have already been mentioned, we start with number three."

"Not so fast", interjected Yohan. "First let us hear the answers to the first questions"

Yeshua replied, giving the answers to his questions one by one.

Question 1 did not mean that YHWH was jealous of some other god. It meant that Israelites should accept that YHWH was the only true God. There were other people who worshipped gods like Baal. YHWH was telling Israel that they should not go after such false gods.

Regarding question 2, the answer was that YHWH endowed man with free will, but wanted total obedience. He planted two special trees in the Garden of Eden, namely the tree of knowledge and the tree of eternal life, but forbade Adam and Eve from eating their fruits. It was a test whether the couple, endowed with free will, would disobey God who asked them not to eat the fruits of the forbidden trees. The result was that they were too easily tempted. Hence they were sent out of Eden to places where such forbidden trees were not available.

Question 3.

How honest were our early Patriarchs? Abraham lied to the Pharaoh that Sarah was his sister and not his wife, with the result that Pharaoh took Sarah into his harem, where she remained for two years. He returned her when he was infected with some itching, which was interpreted as an act of God. In the bargain, Abraham got a lot of presents and became a rich man. He then moved to Palestine and played the same game with King Abimelech, and gained more riches. The next major Patriarch was Jacob. He cheated his father to gain the privileges of the first born son. When Isaac was old and blind, Jacob, with the connivance of his mother, covered his arms and body with goat's skin, and wore his brother's old clothes to smell like him, to fool the bind old man into thinking that he was his elder brother, and thus got the blessings due the first born. Yet YHWH blessed both these cheating Patriarchs.

The answer to this question was that God was dealing with imperfect people and had to choose the best among them. Abraham lived in a community where worship of multiple gods was practiced. He had the courage to leave his native place to worship the one true God. He should not be measured by our current standards. Similarly God chose Jacob as the better of the two brothers. There is nothing great to speak of Esau whose progeny became only a small nation, whereas Jacob's descendents became Israel. God made the right choice in each case.

Q 4: According to the Law given by YHWH to Moses, all male Israelis should be circumcised. But Moses was never circumcised. Why didn't YHWH insist on Moses following the Law.

The answer to this was that Moses did great things for God by leading his people out of Egypt, so an exception could be made for him. God is above the Law.

Q 5 In order to deliver the Promised Land to Israel, God engineered the defeat and slaughter of all the tribes who were occupying Canaan. That is cruelty. It was no fault of the various tribes that they were living in Canaan at that time.

The answer was that nothing survives the wrath of God. If you are on the right side of God you flourish, but if you are on the wrong side you are finished.

Q 6 Jealous God that YHWH was, he wanted Israelis to worship him and offer sacrifices at alters specifically made for that purpose. Does God really want to be worshipped? Isn't it a human weakness to be praised and worshipped?

The answer was that God does not have any weakness for praise, but he wants human beings to grow up with gratitude, a sense of wonder on seeing God's creations and a sense of humility which comes through worship.

Q 7 YHWH is pleased with those who follow his rules, and punishes those who break his statutes. However, he does not seem to do this uniformly. Two outstanding leaders of Israel were King David and his son Solomon. David saw a woman bathing in the neighbourhood. Finding her beautiful, he sent for her immediately and enjoyed sexual relations with her, knowing that she was already married. Later, he got her husband, an army officer, killed treacherously. Solomon had 700 wives and 300 concubines. To support them in their lavish lifestyles, he taxed his people heavily. To please his favourite wives, he built alters for gods of their preference and even joined them in their illegal sacrifices. But YHWH did not punish either of them. He punished their progeny. That does not appear to be a fair way of administering justice.

The answer was that God's time scale was different from ours. Eventually Israel paid for the sins of these rulers; but it should not be forgotten that they made Israel a power to reckon with. These kings got some leeway because they made Israel prosperous and powerful.

B. Authenticity of the Scriptures

It is said that the Torah was written by Moses. In what language did he write it and on what medium (scrolls, tablets etc.)? The only language that was available in the period that Moses lived was the Cuneiform. It was written on unbaked clay and then baked for strength. If the whole of Torah was preserved on clay tablets it would take a hall full of tablets. Further the abstract ideas in Torah could not be expressed in cuneiform. Has anybody seen the written text of the Torah?

Gamaliel did not dispute these arguments, but pointed out that a council of wise men formulated Tanaka around four centuries earlier. He agreed, however, that the written document was not extant. He also admitted that there was general agreement that Tanaka was codified after the Babylonian captivity. He did not dispute the fact that the only written version available was a document in Greek called Septuagint, which goes back only by about 200 years. He saw merit in the argument that recent documents could not be authentic about events that took place more than a millennium earlier.

"What was Rabbi Gamaliel's general response to your questions", asked Yohan.

Yeshua said: "You must remember that Gamaliel is a Rabbi, and cannot agree with me. He gave the standard line that God can make everything possible and that he always acted in Israel's interest. But I felt that he was sympathetic, and regarded my questions as genuine. He called me aside a few times and warned me: 'It is alright to ask me questions, but if you say this publicly you may be hauled before the High Priest for blasphemy".

Yohan asked: "What are your future plans?"

Yeshua: "Rabbi Gamaliel told me that if I wanted to pursue my questions on the nature of God, then I must go to the East. He said that there was a place called Taxila beyond Parthia where there were schools for higher studies in religious thoughts of Buddhists and Hindus. The best way to go there is with a trade caravan that regularly operates between Antioch and Taxila. The Rabbi agreed to give me a letter addressed to a great teacher that he had heard about, but the rest is up to me. The problem is that I do not know how to contact a caravan?"

"Perhaps I can help you there", said Yohan

"Before you proceed further, please tell me what you are doing?" interjected Yeshua.

"I was wondering why you never asked', quipped Yohan. "But let me tell you anyway. I have joined the Essenes".

"I have heard about such a group, but I know hardly anything about them", said Yeshua.

"Well, you know about Sadducees and Pharisees. Essenes are a third Jewish group that is dissatisfied with both of them. Both these groups do not strictly follow the Law. They have compromised their religious beliefs to please the Roman rulers, and for their own monetary gains. Notice how rich these people are. We can regain the lost glory of Israel only if we get rid of these two groups and drive out the Romans as well as their lackeys."

"I have heard it said that the Essenes are revolutionaries", said Yeshua.

"Ignorant people say many things, but we believe that we are the true Israelis", came the sharp reply. "But mark my words! We will triumph in the end, with YAHWEH's help". Yeshua noticed that his cousin's voice rose to a crescendo.

"How do you become an Essene?" asked Yeshua.

"One has to start as a Novice Essene by taking a vow of strict observance of the Law of Moses. There are regular classes held for Novices on the Law and how to adhere to it in practice. These are given by teachers who have a sound knowledge of the Scriptures. In fact, the teachers are trained in our own Training Schools. At the end of two years there is an examination, which along with field reports on adherence of the Law, determines whether you pass the Novice stage. I have passed the Novice course and have become a Deacon."

"What next?"

"I have to serve as a Deacon for five to seven years. This is the time when we learn all the tasks necessary for managing our system. These tasks include cooking and serving food in the dormitories, medical assistance to the sick, organising and managing crowds for meetings and discourses, ensuring cleanliness of dormitories etc."

"Why do you have to manage crowds?" interjected Yeshua.

"Well, there are many people who are interested in attending our meetings, but do not know when and where they are held. Informing them and mobilizing sufficient number of people for our meetings is not a trivial task" replied Yohan "Going back to my main point, it is only after successfully completing this internship do I get a chance to be an Elder".

"What is the advantage of being an Elder?" asked Yeshua.

"Elders form the core group that controls the organisation. The Assembly of Elders elects a Council, which is vested with the powers to take all decisions. The Council is appointed for a period of three years. As the same person can contest elections only for two consecutive terms, there is good rotation of holders of office and there are no hereditary claims. The exception applies only for those who are unanimously elected to executive positions. This is where our administration is superior to that of Sanhedrin."

"Don't you have Priests to officiate at Sacraments?" asked Yeshua.

"Of course, we have. All our elders are trained priests. They are assigned to our synagogues by rotation. We have banned animal sacrifices, which is the main source of corruption in the Jerusalem temple." replied Yohan

"Now let us come to your future plans. I fully support Rabbi Gamaliel's advice that you go to India. A couple of elders that I work with have some contact with a caravan that operates between Antioch and Taxila. I have heard it said that they take young people free, provided you help them with horses and camels, like feeding them and riding them. I will check this and get back to you in a couple of days".

CHAPTER 2

A Caravan Journey to the East

Yohan indeed got back in two days and met his cousin at their favourite meeting place. He brought the news that a caravan that was leaving for Taxila next month had agreed to take Yeshua. In return for the ride, he must ride one of their horses and help to feed and bathe the animals. "But I don't know any horse riding", cried Yeshua. Yohan was ready with his answer. "I have made all the arrangements for that also. On the hills on the opposite side of the Sea of Galilee, we have a training centre. I have arranged for you stay there in a dormitory and learn horse riding. They are confident that they can train you in two weeks". Yohan walked back to Nazareth with his cousin to seek parental permission for the plan. When the matter was presented to Miriam, she was quite upset that her first-born son would be going on a long sojourn to some faraway land. Yohan persuaded her by pointing out that the knowledge that her son was seeking was not available in nearby places. When Yosef came, he also raised objections, but yielded when he found that Yeshua was determined to go.

Early next morning, the two cousins set off to the Essene training centre for Yeshua's training in horse riding. He was a diligent student, who learned quickly, taking full advantage of the opportunities that came his way. He took in his stride the falls from horseback. In two weeks' time the trainer declared that Yeshua had acquired sufficient skill to ride the spare horses in a caravan. "After all, he is not going for horse racing", he quipped.

When the day of departure arrived, Yohan came to escort Yeshua to Damascus and see him off on the caravan. Miriam was weeping, saying that she did not know when she would see her son again. She packed some food consisting of bread and fried fish to last at least a couple of days of the journey. Yosef was busy packing the bags. He accompanied the two boys in their walk to town, where Yohan's friends were waiting to put them on a coach to Damascus. There they had to wait for a day for the caravan.

Yeshua found the caravan journey interesting. Even before the journey started, Yohan introduced him to three people who were Essene sympathizers. One was a trader, and the other two were members of the caravan team, named Andreas and Filipos, The team members turned out to be very helpful, as well as good company. In fact, the trio was often found together and they were generally engaged in serious conversation. The heavy cargo was in cargo vans drawn by camels. The horse-drawn carriages were for traders, some of whom carried costly items with them as personal baggage. Paying passengers also traveled by coach. The others took their position based on their duties. Yeshua's duty was to ride one of the spare horses, as was the case with his two friends. In the event one of the horses drawing the carriages was disabled, the spare horse would replace it. Now the disabled horse had to be looked after until the next watering and resting point. As Arabian horses fetched good prices in the Taxila market, some of them were brought for sale.

Most of the route was through the Parthian Empire. Once the caravan reached the border, Parthian officials came to collect taxes for the use of their territory. The trade route to India and China was a major source of revenue for the State. As the amount of taxes was related to the value of goods, there was much haggling about the value of the goods they were carrying. Since the main purpose of the Eastward Journey was to purchase goods, the cargo was less in this leg of the trip. It also meant that that the caravan could move faster.

Even though paying of taxes was a nuisance, it had some advantages. In order to increase revenue on this account, Parthian authorities set up good infrastructural facilities. These included roads suitable for caravans, wayside inns that provided food and shelter, ferries to go across rivers, and protection against robbers. Yeshua's caravan was accompanied by four armed guards, all of them on horseback. The inns for stopover were contacted by them to make all arrangements like water, food and fodder. More extensive facilities for bathing, washing and drying of clothes, were available near major cities. At such places, an extra day of stay was availed for giving adequate rest for both men and animals. The cities where the caravan stopped for a break were: Seleucia, Ecbatan, Hecatompolice, Merv, and Bactra. Yeshua took advantage of the stopovers for getting some firsthand information about these places. From Bactra the caravan took the Oxus (Amu Darya) valley route to cross the Hindu Khush Mountain, thus minimising the climb. They camped at Bamyian where good facilities were available for caravans. The next day, they proceeded straight to Taxila, except for stop overs for food, water and rest.

Yeshua enjoyed the two-month long journey, though it was arduous. The changing sceneries and different weather conditions attracted his attention. The three friends often discussed such points. As Yeshua was recognized as the more knowledgeable person, he had to answer many questions. Andreas asked the first question. "Why does it get cooler as we go to higher and higher altitudes? As we climb to higher levels, we are going closer to the sun, which is the source of heat and light. Therefore, it should get hotter as we climb up. In actual fact it gets cooler. How do you explain it?" Yeshua had his answer: "A few thousand cubits that we have climbed is negligibly small compared to the distance to the sun and this contributes very little to the change in temperature. The important factor is that the mountainside is sloping. Therefore, the heat and light that falls on a patch of land on the plains, falls on a larger area on the mountain, reducing the heat per unit area. Less heat means lower temperature. Filipos asked the next question. "Why is it colder at night than during day time?" "The answer to that is easy", said Yeshua, "At night there is no sun. So we do not get sun's light or heat. Therefore the temperature is lower".

The next question was about the four seasons. "What causes the change of seasons? Why is it hot in the summer and cold in the winter?"

Yeshua: "Seasons are caused by the tilt of the earth from its orbit. Eratosthenese, the Greek mathematician, measured this tilt as 23.5 degrees from the perpendicular to the orbit by an elegant experiment. Because of this tilt, the sun at noon appears directly above the equator twice in a year, once at the beginning of spring and another at the beginning of autumn. The spring sun moves north until it reaches 23.5 degrees from the equator, to begin the summer. Then it moves back to the equator marking the beginning of autumn. It continues its southern journey, reaching the southern limit of 23.5 degrees when winter starts. In another three months it reaches the equator. That is when the Romans celebrate the winter solstice. The whole cycle is repeated every year. Thus we have four seasons. As we live north of the 23.5 degree limit, we never see the sun directly overhead even at noon. It is important to realize that the sun actually does not move north and south. It is the tilt of the earth that makes it appear to do that." As his companions found it difficult to comprehend it, Yeshua had to draw a diagram in sand to explain it to them.

Then came the next question: "What causes eclipses?" Yeshua explained it to them. "While the earth rotates around the sun, the moon rotates around the earth. During these rotations, there are occasions when the moon comes between the sun and the earth. This blocking of the sun by the moon is known as solar eclipse when the sun is invisible to us partially or wholly. There are other occasions when the earth comes between the sun and the moon. As moon is visible to us only when the sun shines on it, earth's blocking of sunlight makes the moon invisible to us partially or wholly. This is known as lunar eclipse." His friends were very impressed by the way Yeshua could explain all these by physical principles, while most people had to invoke God to explain these phenomena. But Andreas had a doubt. "In the Book of Joshua, it is said that the sun stood still until Joshua's army finished off the Amorites at Gideon. How do you explain this in the light of your scientific knowledge?" Yeshua said: "This story is just an exaggeration. The author of the book obviously did not witness the event. When you say that the sun stood still in the sky, it means that the earth stopped its rotation on its axis, making the sun to appear to stand still. This requires enormous amount of energy and its consequences have to be analyzed by experts. Such an action assumes that God, who presides over all the countless stars that you see above, stop the spin of our planet to ensure the death of a large number of Amorites. The statement in the Book of Joshua should caution us against a literal acceptance of the Scripture"'

Yeshua turned out to be a very valuable member of the caravan team. His knowledge of both Aramaic and Greek was very useful at border check posts. He was quite active during the breaks in the journey, feeding animals, serving food and making sure that everybody had a place to rest or sleep. His Essene friends were equally active. In fact the trio made a good team. The traders who were managing the caravan noticed this, and made a mental note to add Yeshua to their team. After a long caravan trip, they finally reached Taxila. Though they reached their destination very late, the facilities there were excellent. Man and beast rested for three days, enjoying the food, the scenery and the dips in the crystal clear waters of the tributaries of Indus. Though Yeshua could leave the caravan now, the rest of the group had business to do. They had to sell the cargo that they brought and buy the cargo to take back with them. Of course, there were cargo agents to help.

Taxila was a city between the rivers Sindhu, called Indus by the Greek, and Hydaspes. Its northern limit was the Haro River, and on the south it was bounded by Margala Hills. The name Taxila itself was the Greek version of Takshasila, a city dating back to the Gandhara period. The city was built on the banks of Tamra Nala, a rivulet which ends in Haro River, which in turn was a tributary of Indus. It was a great centre of learning for over six hundred years before Yeshva arrived there.

The importance and prosperity of Taxila arose from its strategic location at the junction of three great highways: 1. The *uttarapada,* the Royal High Road linking Gandhara in the west with Pataliputhra, the capital of Magadh, in the East. 2. The north western route to Bactra and thence to the Mediterranean Sea and Rome by the Silk Road. 3. The Indus valley route which linked the Arabian Sea with Kashmir through Taxila, and from there connected to the Silk Road going to China. This made Taxila a transfer and trade centre for goods, and a resting place for caravans.

About 500 years earlier this place was known as Takshashila, the capital of Gandhara. According the Indian epic *Ramayana,* Takshashila was founded by Bharatha, the younger brother of Lord Rama, and was named after Bharatha's son Taksha, who became its first ruler. Later Gandhara became a satrapy of the Persian King Darius. About 300 years before the events described here, Alexander the Great invaded India and the then ruler of Taxila, King Ambhi; presented the territory to him. Alexander died five years later, and shortly thereafter, Chandragupta Maurya, the ruler of Magadha annexed Taxila to his Kingdom. His grandson Ashoka made Taxila into a Buddhist centre of learning, and built monasteries and stupas to propagate Buddha's message. After Ashoka's period, Taxila went into the hands of Indo - Greek rulers of Bactria. When Yeshua arrived in Taxila, it was the capital of the Indo-Partian Kingdom and the reigning King was Gondophares.

Tamra Nala was a meandering stream, which originated in the Margala hills on the South of Taxila. After flowing for a short distance in the northwest direction, the stream veered west and then started flowing north, and then turned west again and continued its zig zag flow until it reached Haro River. Taxila was built on the right side of the north - south section of Tamra Nala. The city of Gandharas was said to be buried under the Bhir mound which was visible on the left bank where the stream started flowing north. Further north, but on the opposite bank was situated Sirkap, the capital city built by the Indo - Greek kings. The current Monarch Gondophares lived here. The monasteries were farther east, and the university was in between. The caravan that brought Yeshua was in the Caravan Sanctuary which was located on the left bank of Tamra Nala, a little downstream from Sirkap.

A couple of days after they arrived in Taxila, the Jewish trader named Yosef sent for Yeshua. He said: "Yeshua, I have been watching you throughout this trip. You have done a good job, and we would like to offer you regular job on the caravan. However, I realise that you are slated for bigger things. So I will pay you a few gold coins, which may be useful to you to pay Guru Dakshina when you start your studies. Further, the horses that you and your friends were riding are going to be sold in a couple of days, and I will pay you a few more gold coins." "Thank you, sir", said Yeshua. "I was expecting only the ride. But I greatly appreciate your generosity, as it will help me with tuition fees in this university." Yosef continued: "Tomorrow I am going to make a courtesy call on King Gondophares. We traders have to keep the authorities in good humour. You may accompany me then. I think it may turn out to be useful to have an introduction to the King."

The next day Yeshua accompanied Yosef to the Royal Palace. A servant followed them with a large case. Seeing the expression of surprise on his companion's face, Yosef explained: "It is customary to carry a present when you go to meet the King. This is a case of the best Palestinian wine. In fact, wine is one of the merchandises that I have brought, as it fetches a good price here." An attendant ushered them into a hall where the King met visitors. They did not have to wait long, as the king was known to be punctual in meeting visitors. As they were ushered into their seats, the King said: "Welcome, welcome, honoured guest. We are happy to receive guests like you who bring more revenue to our treasury. Is it the fine Palestinian wine that you brought as gift? As you know, I drink very little, but your supply will be gone in no time, when I hold a reception". "Your Majesty is very gracious as usual. The infrastructural facilities that you have set up are so good that we keep coming back", said Yosef. "Is this young man your new associate?" asked the King. "This is Yeshua who wants to study in your great university"', "Welcome, young man", said the King. "I like young people who travel such long distances to study. They add to the culture as well as the quest of knowledge that the university stands for. For example, most people are so used to their own laws and practices that they are not even aware of other systems and societies. I am sure that your presence will enrich Taxila University. Are you supporting his education, Yosef?". "I have the impression that he would rather not depend on me or anybody else for support. He wants to work to pay for his education", replied Yosef. "It is not as easy as you think. I cannot be of much help to you in this matter, as the university is autonomous, and even the King does not interfere in academic matters. However, one possibility comes to my mind. A group of traders want a course in Aramaic, so that they can deal with authorities at border check posts and markets in Parthia and Palestine. If you are proficient in Aramaic, we can consider you for the teacher's post. Of course, you have to meet the university's requirements. If you are selected, it will suit you well, as anyway you may have to join the school of languages first to gain proficiency in Pali. So you can teach Aramaic to earn your living expenses and learn Pali in evening classes". "I will consider myself blessed if I get this position", interjected Yeshua.

"I wish you success, young man", said the King, "Let me add something more. If you succeed and earn a high grade from the Acharya of the Language School, you can apply for a State Scholarship. As I said, the State does not interfere in academic affairs. But we give financial support. This may be in the form of buildings, salaries of faculty or scholarships awarded to bright students who have no other support. I would be happy if you get one of these scholarships". Yeshua thanked the King profusely, as what the king had indicated was a lot more than what he had expected.

As they walked out of the Palace, Yosef told Yeshua that the caravan would continue to be in the present shelter until all the goods they brought were sold and the merchandise for the return trip were purchased. This could take a minimum of one week, perhaps even two or three weeks. Yeshua could continue to stay in the shelter. "Actually, I was thinking of paying your tuition. But what you are getting is better", Yosef said. Yeshua thanked him, but felt happy that he did not have to impose so much on the generosity of this kind man. He obtained permission to look around the place. First he walked around Sirkap and noticed its Greek architecture, with rectangular buildings built with stone blocks on streets laid out on a grid pattern. His next destination was the university. It was a collection of schools dealing with different subjects such as medicine, arthashasthra (economics), politics, religion (Vedas, Buddhism), military science and languages. Each was headed by an Acharya (Dean) who was always a well known scholar. Each school had its buildings with class rooms in the centre, surrounded by residential rooms. Each of these building clusters had mess facilities as well as quarters for teachers.

In the days that followed Yeshua was tested for his proficiency in Aramaic and, finding him way ahead of other candidates, the authorities offered him the post of temporary teacher. This assured him of a room to stay in, and food from the mess. In addition, he would get a modest sum of money paid in gold coins. Yosef stayed on until Yeshua was settled in his new residence. When the time came to say goodbye, Yosef settled Yeshua's account and paid him for his services in the caravan and with the horse. In addition Yosef paid him a part of the profit he got by selling the Arabian horse that Yeshua was riding. "I don't need this now", protested Yeshua. "These are your dues", said Yosef. "You may need it in future. I will be coming here with my caravan once in a few months. I can then carry all the news about you to your parents and friends. I have heard a lot about you from your cousin Yohan. Perhaps you may also have heard about me. Back home, I am known as Yosef of Arimathea". "Of course I have heard that name. Yohan has told me how helpful you are. But I didn't realise that I was traveling with the same person all this time. Thank you, sir, for all that you have done for me and for Yohan", replied Yeshua. "We have great expectations from you, Yeshua", said Yosef cryptically and walked off.

Yeshua moved into his room in the Language School, and put all his effort into teaching of Aramaic. The library in the language school was a great help. The scrolls were well arranged and classified. His students were grown men with trade interests in Parthia and Palestine. They were initially skeptical about the ability and knowledge of this young boy. But as the classes proceeded, all their doubts vanished. Yeshua answered all their questions patiently. If there was anything for which he could not give an answer immediately, he would go and search in the library in the evening, and give his answer the next day. He became very popular with his students, and some of them asked his help for their routine work. He readily agreed, but when they insisted on paying, he sought the advice of the Acharya. The Acharya told him that he was earning by doing this work in his spare time, and he was entitled to keep it. Yeshua explained to his class that Aramaic was a language spoken in a large area from

Parthia to Palestine. So there are local variations called dialects. He explained how dialects changed from one area to another. This was a great help to traders who had to travel to different places.

When the Aramaic classes were running smoothly, Yeshua joined the evening classes for Pali. The introductory course was given by Shakuntala, the daughter of Guru Sahadeva, the Acharya of the School of Languages. She was doing it as part of her teacher training course. She explained that Pali was the language in which Buddhist Dharma was popularised. Pali was written in Brahmi script, which could be seen in many parts of the subcontinent including the South. Pali was spoken and understood all over the North from Magadh in the east to Taxila in the west. As Yeshua joined her classes later than others, he was required to make up for the lost classes. Shakuntala suggested that they do it whenever she had free time. She was happy to do this because this young foreigner was so focused on his studies. She noticed that Yeshua had problem with the Brahmi script, which was different from the scripts that he was familiar with. By persistence he mastered the script. A few meetings were sufficient to convince Shakuntala that she was dealing with an exceptionally bright student. She reported this to her father, and held the next session at home so that the Acharya could meet the new find. Guru Sahadeva confirmed his daughter's observation, but advised against taking any immediate action, as Yeshua was earning while learning. When Yeshua finished Shakunthala's preliminary course with ease, he was put on the next level course, which normally took two years. When he finished this course in time, he had already gained a good working knowledge of Pali. Guru Sahadeva decided to extend the course by six months so that Yeshua became quite proficient in Pali. The Guru then called him for a meeting to decide his future course of study. Yeshua was very clear about his goal. He came to Taxila to study Buddhism. Therefore, he was sent to the Guru in charge of Studies on Buddhism. Acharya Shantideva said he would be happy to give Yeshua admission, but he must apply for King's Scholarship. The application went to the King with recommendations from both the Acharyas. The King remembered meeting the applicant with Yosef of Arimathea, and sanctioned the scholarship for the full period of study.

As he had a few days before classes started, Yeshua decided to go on a tour to see the University and its surrounding areas. Shakuntala offered to show him around the campus. They walked around looking at the buildings that housed various Schools, like the School of Religion where Yeshua would spend the next seven years. She explained to him that each School was headed by an Acharya, while every teacher was referred to as Guru. As they passed the School of Medicine, she pointed out that this was the School which was once presided over by Charaka, the famous physician, "whose pioneering work in medicine was done right here". She also proudly pointed out that her father was now the Acharya of the School of Languages, where Panini once developed his treatise on Sanskrit grammar. *However, the old structures broke down and were replaced by new buildings after my father was appointed Acharya. One of the best known products of Taxila,* she said, *was Chanakya who graduated from this University more than three centuries ago. He later became an Acharya in Economics and Political Science. His book Arthasastra was still considered one of the greatest treatises on the subject. He was most famous as the political advisor of Chandragupta Maurya I who became King of Magadha because of his clever moves. He later became advisor to Chandragupts's son Bindusara, who succeeded his father on the throne of Magadha. During Chanakya's time the University was very famous for Martial Arts and Political Science. Most of the royal families sent their princes here for training.* Shakuntala also showed her companion the location where Alexander the Great camped when he conquered India. They then looked at the temples at the east end of the campus. Their tour then took them to the other side of Tamra Nala, to cross which they had to walk on a single-plank wooden bridge. Seeing Shakuntala's anxiety about slipping and falling into the water, Yeshua offered his hand which she held until they reached the other end. It was a pleasant sensation for Yeshua. On the opposite bank, they went to the Bhir Mound underneath which the remains of more ancient times were buried. On the return trip, Shakuntala suggested that they go further north and take a broader bridge to cross the river. But Yeshua pointed out that it was getting dark and advised her to use the same one-plank bridge. He put his arm around her and guided her to the other side. Shakuntala did not complain about this proximity. It was sunset when Yeshua dropped her off at her residence.

CHAPTER 3

Study of Buddhism in Taxila University

Yeshua enrolled to study Buddhism under Acharya Shantideva in the School of Studies in Religion. He realised that Shantideva was one of the top scholars on the subject, and an ordained monk. Being the senior most Acharya in Taxila University, he had also many management responsibilities. Yeshua learned that Buddhism was the practice of Buddha's teachings which were called Dharma. Buddha lived in North Eastern Bharth [India] about six centuries before Yeshua's period. He was born as Siddhartha Gauthama, son of King Suddhodana who ruled over the Sakhya Kingdom. Soon after Prince Gauthama was born, an astrologer predicted that the child would be either a great king or renounce the material world to become a holy man. The King wanted only the former option, and hence young Gauthama was confined to the palace in Kapilavastu, and grew up without any contact with the outside world. The King made sure that his son was provided with all the luxuries befitting his royal status. When he was twenty nine years old, Gauthama ventured out, on his own, beyond the palace gates and learned about the suffering of ordinary people. The four sights that he saw - an old man, a sick man, a corpse and an ascetic who looked contended and at peace – left a profound impression on him. The first two sights made him aware of the sufferings in this world, the third sight showed that human beings exist in this world only for a limited period and the last one indicated that one can be contended with limited worldly possessions. He then left the palace under cover of darkness, leaving behind his pretty wife and child, and started his spiritual journey. He learned the Vedas and tried extreme asceticism through which he almost starved to death, His companions left him thinking he was dead. A village girl passing by noticed that he was alive and fed him some milk, and thus brought him back to life. He then practiced meditation and arrived at the Middle Way between self-indulgence and self-mortification.

Siddhartha Gowthama continued his meditation under a pepal tree (*Bodhi* tree), determined to continue it until he found his answers. On the 49th day he attained enlightenment and became Buddha. In a flash he got a profound insight into human suffering and the steps necessary to put an end to it. He went to Banaras and began his teaching. Buddhists call his teachings Dharma. Buddha is believed to have turned the wheel of Dharma at Banaras. He continued teaching till the age of eighty. During this period he gave 84000 teachings, which constitute the Dharma that his followers practice. A Buddhist is one who practices Dharma.

The essence of Buddhism is contained in the Four Noble Truths that Buddha revealed to his followers in the very first discourse he gave after attaining enlightenment. They are the truth of suffering, the truth of the cause of suffering, the truth of the end of suffering, and the truth of the path that leads to the end of suffering. Suffering is the lot of all beings, who are caught in *samsara,* the cycle of birth and rebirth governed by the rules of Karma. Karma is not fate or predestination. The word Karma itself means action, which produces its effect. Just as a tree which we plant yields tasty or bitter fruits, depending on the nature of the tree, our actions give rise to happiness or suffering depending on whether those actions are righteous or unrighteous. Our good, wholesome or righteous actions give fruits which give happiness, whereas our unrighteous actions yield fruits of sorrow when they ripen. This is called *karma phala* – fruit of karma. Only intentional, deliberate, conscious actions would produce fruits. It may not be known to us when the fruits would ripen – it may be in the present birth but it can also be in a later birth. At the end of our lives when consciousness leaves the current body and finds a new host, the karma account is carried forward. In fact, the choice of the new host itself is based on the karma score. Actions that would cause the ripening of bitter fruits are tenfold: three originating from our body, four from our speech [or mouth] and three from our mind. Unwholesome actions coming from our body are: killing, stealing and sexual misconduct. They cause physical harm to the adversary. Bad action emanating through our mouths are: lying, slander, harsh speech and malicious gossip. These cause emotional harm to the target. Unrighteous actions originating from our minds are: greed, anger and delusions. These cause physical, mental and emotional damage to the affected beings. If we can avoid these ten types of actions, there will be no fruit of suffering on account of our actions.

All human beings crave for pleasure and are engaged in the pursuit of acquiring wealth and in the satisfaction of their sensual needs. This is responsible for their bad actions, which enhances their suffering throughout their lives and in future births as well. These sufferings may be due to illness, not getting what one craves for, losing a dear object or person, or old age and death. At the end the worldly life, such people have a low Karma score with the result they are born into a lower form of life. The Karma score is the algebraic sum of the effects of the wholesome as well as unwholesome acts not only in the current life but also in the countless lives the person had lived in his or her previous births.

There are six different planes into which any living being can be reborn - three fortunate and three unfortunate realms. Those with positive karma are reborn into the fortunate realms of men, demigods, and gods. Those with negative karma are reborn as animals, hungry ghosts and hell beings. Of the six realms, Hell Beings are the worst off. It is said that there are hot and cold cells in Hell and the hell beings suffer from extreme hot and cold conditions. The causes by which sentient beings end up in this state are habitual killing and cruelty. However in Buddhism, there is no eternal damnation. When their unwholesome karma is exhausted after the prescribed period of stay in hell, these hell beings are born into higher realms. Hungry Ghosts come next in the order of suffering. They suffer hunger and thirst all the time, and are totally bereft of objects of their desire. The causes for their condition are avarice and miserliness born out of greed. The third is the realm of Animals, who live in fear and pain because they can be killed and eaten by other animals. They are also butchered by human beings for food, or else used as beasts of burden. The causes which brought them to this realm are ignorance and blind pursuit of desires. The most fortunate of the six realms is that of gods [*devas*]. They are the happiest because they have the possibility of enjoying sensual as well as spiritual pleasures or tranquility. However, they get distracted by the former and have little time for tranquility. When their wholesome Karma is exhausted, they are born into a lower realm. The next most fortunate realm is that of demi-gods [*asuras*]. Asuras are more intelligent and physically more powerful than humans, but suffer from jealousy and conflict. They are envious of gods and pride is their weakness. When they exhaust their good Karma score, they get reborn into a lower realm.

There is suffering in all these realms, but human beings are fortunate as they have a way out of *samsara*. They can break the endless cycle of rebirth by following Buddha Dharma, which starts with the four golden truths. The first three of the four golden truths assert that there is suffering, points out the causes of this condition, and assures us that it is possible to end this suffering both in this world and later. The fourth truth tells us the steps one has to take to end the suffering. Buddha has charted out an eight fold noble path to achieve this goal.

The eight fold Noble Path was realised and taught by Buddha as the only way to achieve *Nirvana*, the state of supreme happiness. It consists of:

1. RIGHT VIEW. Right view or Right Perspective or Perfect Vision is based on an understanding of the Noble Truths. It includes the acceptance of the principle of Karma - that 'all beings are the owners of their actions; whatever deeds they do, good or bad, they shall be heirs of'.

2. RIGHT INTENTION or Right Resolve is being resolved on renunciation, on freedom from ill will, on harmlessness and on a commitment to non-violence. It is the intention to renounce worldly things that helps the practitioner to resist the pull of craving which is the root cause of suffering. It is the intention of goodwill that leads to selfless love for all other beings. It is the intention of harmlessness that leads to universal compassion.

3. RIGHT SPEECH means abstaining from telling lies, slander, harsh or hurtful language, and idle chatter.

4. RIGHT ACTION or Integral Action is ethical action based on the principle of non-exploitation of oneself and others. It includes abstaining from killing, stealing and sexual misconduct. Abstaining from killing also means exclusion of the benefits of killing and therefore a Buddhist avoids non-vegetarian food.

5. RIGHT LIVELIHOOD is livelihood based on the ethical principle of non-exploitation. This means earning ones living in a righteous way:

legally, honestly, peacefully, and without causing harm or suffering to others.

6. RIGHT EFFORT or Right Endeavour is the persistent effort to give up all wrong or harmful thoughts, words and actions; abandoning any such unwholesome mental states that may have been aroused; persisting in giving rise to mental states that are good for themselves and others; and maintaining such wholesome mental states.

7. RIGHT MINDFULNESS: "Dharma, the ultimate truth is not something mysterious and remote, but the truth of our own experience. It has to be known by our own insight. What brings the field of experience into focus and makes it accessible to insight is mindfulness or awareness." Awareness is realised through contemplation of the body, feelings, states of mind and phenomena.

8. RIGHT CONCENTRATION makes the mind still and steady, opening vast vistas of bliss, serenity and power. It helps the practitioner to generate insights which unveil the ultimate truth of things. Concentration is developed through meditation.

Yeshua soon realised that Buddha's Dharma was not open for debate. A Buddhist, he understood, was one who accepted it and practiced it. The only discussion was on how to practice Dharma. Yeshua had no problem in accepting that there was suffering in this world. That the cause of all suffering was our own delusion was a proposition that he was willing to examine. It was quite true that our attachment to the pleasures of this world, our clinging to material possessions, and our attachments to those whom we like could lead to our suffering or our unhappiness. If our favourite pleasures are denied to us we feel unhappy. If our material possessions are taken from us, we feel miserable. If we lose our dear ones, either through death or disaffection, we feel depressed. That these miseries could be the result of sins committed in a previous birth is something he found difficult to accept, particularly because his own religion or community did not recognise rebirth. It was also intellectually unacceptable. How can his mind, with all the linguistic and theological knowledge, fit into the brain of an ant, in the event he became an ant in the next birth. However, the idea that one was responsible for the consequences of ones own actions appealed to him. An end to the suffering of every being was very desirable. On the other hand, that Buddha's eightfold noble path was the only way to end all suffering was an absolute statement that could not be tested. There could be other paths. All he could do was to test whether this prescription worked.

Yeshua, therefore, decided to plunge himself into the task of following the eightfold Noble Path. He was not alone, as there were many fellow students at various stages of practice. Simultaneously, he enrolled in Yoga classes, because it was said to give the physical and mental discipline necessary for concentration and meditation. It was Yoga that gave first positive results. Yeshua found his body becoming more supple and flexible, and his mind becoming more controlled and fit for concentration and meditation. He found that the lotus posture was the most suited for meditation. Absence of non-vegetarian food did not pose a problem. Anyway, only vegetarian food was available on campus.

The first two factors of the eight fold noble path dealt with wisdom, a conceptual understanding of reality as it actually was, not as seen through the prism of delusion. The right view was an understanding of how reality worked. It brought to focus the human condition - the suffering from birth, and continuing with ageing, sickness and death. It recognised the existence of greed, grasping attachment, hatred and delusion which cloud our eyes and blur our vision. The right view also tells us that there could be an end for this suffering and pointed out a way to achieve it. Right intention was the resolve to renounce worldly possessions and pleasures, and their grip on us. It also meant a firm commitment to rid ourselves of ill will, hatred and anger, but instead cultivate harmlessness, universal love and compassion. Yeshua spent considerable time contemplating these points, frequently examining himself for any traces of undesirable thoughts or desires.

The next three factors came under the category of ethical conduct. Right speech was about being truthful in what we spoke and avoiding talks which were harmful or hurtful to others. Right action eschewed exploitation of others. Obviously, killing, stealing and sexual misconduct were not acceptable. Right livelihood was earned in the righteous way, without causing harm or hardship to others. Yeshua had no problem with these ethical factors, as he was already living an ethical life.

The next three factors were concerned with *samadhi* or concentration. This was to be achieved through training in higher consciousness which brought the calm and collectedness needed to develop true wisdom by direct experience. Right effort required constant monitoring of thoughts and actions, and mental states. Unwholesome ones were not allowed to rise, and wholesome ones were retained. Right mindfulness or awareness was the contemplation of ones body, feelings, state of mind, as well as all the phenomena that affected us. This was necessary to ensure that we progressed in the right direction. Right concentration was the control of the mind. A still and steady mind was required to achieve bliss and serenity. It was in this state that ultimate truths got revealed. To achieve this state, much meditation and practice were required. The Eight Fold Noble Path has been compared to the climbing of a tall hill. At the bottom itself one should have a clear view of the goal, which is to reach the top. It is this view that gives the climber the right intention to reach the top. Only those who practice the proper ethical conduct would be going in the right direction to the top. Only those who have the ability to concentrate single-mindedly on climbing to the top will reach there. As with mountain climbing, there is the risk slipping down at every step of the way. But with concentration and mindfulness, those who are determined get to the top.

The going was tough in the beginning, as Yeshua found his mind wandering off from the rigid requirement of the practitioner of Dharma. But slowly he gained control of his mind. He was able to follow the eight fold noble path. He found that it was continuous practice that was the trick. He had to learn Buddha's *sutras* to recite as he practiced. Gradually Yeshua started enjoying the practice. He realised that he could view his body and mind and the processes they were going through as if he was standing outside. The very fact that he could observe his thought processes from outside brought these thoughts under control. However, it took months and months of practice before he could reach the stage of samadhi. It was a great feeling to know that he could detach himself from worldly possessions and pleasures, and even from his own thought processes.

Yeshua also joined the chant sessions, when the whole group of students repeated the Pali chant:

Buddham saranam gacchami
Dharmam saranam gacchami
Sangham saranam gacchami
This meant:
To Buddha I go for refuge
To Dharma I go for refuge
To Sangham I go for refuge

Here Buddha stands for enlightenment, Dharma stands for Buddha's teachings and Sangha represents the community of Buddhists who sustains each other in their faith, not letting one to slip back. Yeshua enjoyed the chant sessions and realized that it had its role in practicing Buddhism.

Shakuntala periodically dropped in to School of Religion to enquire how Yeshua was doing. This was easy for her as she was giving some lectures on Vedic Hinduism as part of the course in Buddhism. She was a source of encouragement to Yeshua who was living in a foreign land far away from relatives and friends. As she came after the daytime classes, Yeshua went out for walks with her on the campus. Sometimes the walks would end up in her house, where she would treat him with tea and snacks. Yeshua found out that Shakuntala was not only teaching Vedic Hinduism, but also writing a treatise on that subject. On one of his visits he met Acharya Sahadeva who wanted Yeshua's help in starting a course in Aramaic. He said that there were requests for it from the trading community who were willing to support the course financially. "Shakuntala can handle it, as she knows Aramaic. She often speaks to me in Aramaic", opined Yeshua. The Guru's answer was: "If it becomes a regular feature, she should take the responsibility. But to start with, she wants you to be associated with the course". Yeshua agreed to this arrangement, particularly because the classes were planned to be held in the evenings. Further this brought Yeshua in regular contact with Shakuntala which was what both of them wanted. In addition, the Jewish teacher added value to the course as reflected in the enrolment.

Meanwhile, Yeshua did not neglect the regular course of study that he was undergoing along with other students. However, more interesting to him was the opportunity to interact personally with Acharya Shanthideva. In the very first session itself Yeshua asked his basic question. "Buddha's Dharma is based on the concept of *samsara*, in which transmigration of the soul and the transfer of the Karma score from one birth to the next, are fundamental assumptions. Is there any proof for these assumptions?" The Guru answered: "First of all, let me tell you that Buddhists do not believe in transmigration of souls. Buddha taught us that when we die our consciousness, which is the indestructible part of every being, finds another host depending on our Karma. So let me answer your question, assuming that you are referring to this process. My answer to one of your fellow students would be that we should not question Buddha's

Dharma. But I realise that you have come from a different religion which does not teach *samsara*. So let me answer your question this way: Your question is like asking for proof for the existence of God. I would say that rather than ask for proof for God's existence, you should experience God. The same is the case with Dharma. You practice Dharma and enjoy permanent peace of mind. If you want a more intellectual answer, I would say: 'If there is no God, how would you explain the existence of the universe, the countless stars, all the flora and fauna? There has to be a creator and sustainer'. Similarly I do not know a better way to escape the sufferings in *samsara* than through Dharma." Later Yeshua asked his next question: "The human population of earth has been increasing every year. Where do you get spirits or rather consciousnesses for the additional babies who are born every year?" Shanthideva dismissed the question with ease. He asked: "Who said you need more human consciousnesses? The earth and the oceans have been full of sentient beings from the beginning. Has anybody kept count of them to say that they are not enough?"

In a later session, Yeshua asked another question. "Sir, you told me that each one of us had countless lives before the present one, and may have countless lives yet to come. On this timescale why is there so much emphasis on undergoing all this practice in our short life, which is only a small fraction of the continuing process? "Buddha himself has answered this question", said the Guru. "We are fortunate to be born human beings in this life. This is because human beings have a way out of *samsara*. Animals cannot practice Dharma. Buddha explained the situation with an example. Imagine a large ocean of the size of our earth. Now think of a blind turtle that lives at the bottom of the ocean. Imagine also a golden yoke floating on the surface of this ocean. If the blind turtle has the chance of coming to the surface once in hundred thousand years, what are its chances of reaching the golden yoke and putting its head through the middle yoke? Similar is our chance of being born as human beings. So this life is indeed precious. It should not be wasted in pursuing illusive pleasures. It should be used to find permanent liberation from suffering". In another session, Yeshua asked a new question:"There are many religions in the world. The principal ones that I am familiar with are Judaism, Buddhism and Hinduism. All of them have their own beliefs and theology. All of them claim that their way is superior. How can I judge which is true and which is not?" Shanthideva answered the question readily. "Buddha himself has answered this question. He said that you should not accept any teaching because it comes from an authority, nor because it is written down. You should not accept it because of reverence to the teacher, or because it sounds reasonable. You should verify it by testing it yourself in the light of your experience. Then you can eliminate what is harmful and adopt what is beneficial. For example, if you act with greed and anger, it will lead to a disturbed state of mind and hence to suffering. If you eliminate greed and anger from your mind, you will experience calm and happiness. Similarly, you can test other teachings and accept whatever is best for you, based on your own experience." Yeshua acknowledged that his questions were answered.

Acharya Shanthideva explained that "the world we see around us is not real. It is just an illusion. It appears to us as real because of our delusions. For countless lives, sentient beings have been busy chasing their pleasures. The more they go after pleasures, the more they are miserable. The real cause of the problem is people's attachment to their possessions and affections. In order to acquire and retain them, people get angry, fight, and do many undesirable things, which condemn them to misery not only in their present lives, but also in many future lives. The root cause of this condition is our greed which stems from ignorance, giving us a distorted view of the world. As a result we don't know what is real and what is illusory. The first step in getting out of this ignorance is to understand that whatever we see as attractive in this world is the creation of our mind. It is just appearance, not reality. Without the prism of our distorting mind, the world is empty. When you begin to practice Dharma, you should train your mind to seek this emptiness."

"Gouthama Buddha taught his Dharma through Suktas. In the Sukta of the four noble truths, he told us that we should experience suffering. In fact, the first noble truth is that there is suffering. For any living being there is suffering from birth to death. Birth itself brings suffering to both the child and the mother. The new born baby cries most of the time, indicating that he/she is uncomfortable. Then there is sickness which we get subjected to. Any illness saps our energy and causes physical discomfort. As we grow older we have much work to do to support ourselves and our dependents, which appears like a big burden to us. As we get still older, our muscles get weaker making it difficult to perform even our normal functions. What Buddha told us is that unless we suffer, we will not get the strong desire to put an end to it. It is not enough to get temporary relief for ourselves in the present life. We want to avoid suffering in countless future lives and we want it for all people and all sentient beings for all time. Only if we contemplate on this will we move forward on the eightfold noble path eventually to reach *nirvana*."

"Meditating on death is encouraged in Buddhism. Death is certain, only its time remains uncertain. If we are going to die, what is the use of all the possessions and power that we have accumulated over a lifetime? What is even more significant is that in Buddhist theology impermanence [*anithya*] is linked to suffering [*dukha*] and not-self [*anatma*]. Buddha has said that whatever is impermanent is suffering, and whatever is impermanent and suffering is also not-self. In our ignorance of the real nature of things, we crave for and cling to impermanent attributes like youth, health and life, in the hope that they will give us permanent happiness. Once they end, we revert to unhappy states."

"*Anatma* or impersonality or not-self is a distinctly Buddhist concept. Buddha has stated that the term 'I' does not stand for any essence or entity. He explained it with the example of a chariot. If you look for a chariot among its parts, you don't find it. A chariot is not its wheels, or its axle or the carriage. It is a convenient name given for the collection of parts fitted together in a particular way. In the same way, if we look for self or 'I' in our body we cannot locate it. The head is not self, nor is the heart or the limbs or any other organ. The mind is also not self, as it is not in our control, but jumps around like a monkey. We may conclude that self is not to be found in the body or in the mind." Yeshua now asked his next question: "Guruji, in the very beginning of the course I was taught that I am the owner of my actions and their consequences. I am also owner of my meager belongings like my body, my clothes and the knowledge most of which I have gained here. If I don't exist, how can I be the owner of these things?" "This is not what Buddha meant by self. He was referring to those people who think that self is an independent, permanent entity", replied Shantideva. "It is because of this notion of permanence that people accumulate possessions, build big mansions and cling on to them. It is because of this concept of 'I' that people try to dominate over others. This is also the reason why they crave for pleasures. The moment we bring in the 'I' factor, we are erecting a barrier between ourselves and others. We end up defending ourselves, our positions and our possessions, thereby creating many enemies. On the other hand, if we abandon the notion of self, our delusions disappear. Through the understanding of impermanence, suffering and not-self, we get rid of our fundamental errors of seeing things as permanent, as pleasant and as self. When these delusions are removed, wisdom dawns on us and we are on the threshold of nirvana."

"In order to appreciate it better, we can go back to Buddha's Middle Way, which he arrived at after his initial penance. When this concept was introduced, we explained it as avoidance of the extremes of self mortification and self indulgence in pleasure. But it can also be applied to the understanding of *anatma* [not-self]. Buddha never rejected the idea of 'I' altogether. He pointed out the danger of imagining that our personality is a permanent, independent entity. That is the Middle Way between its total rejection under all circumstances, and clinging on to it as a permanent entity. Affirming the existence of an independent, permanent self is eternalism. The opposite of this is nihilism, which denies any correlation between action and its consequences. While eternalism pushes us deeper into *samsara,* nihilism closes the door for liberation from it. The Middle Way would avoid these two extremes, thus enabling us to reach eternal happiness by following Dharma. It may be noted that Buddha developed his teachings with great care. Buddha's teachings have been likened to approach of a tigress to her young cub. When the tigress carries her baby by holding it between her teeth, she is careful to ensure that the grip is neither too tight nor too loose. If the grip is too tight on the neck, it could injure the cub. If the grip is too loose, the cub could fall down. Buddha's teachings help us to avoid the extremes of eternalism and nihilism, as also the extremes of self mortification and worldly pleasures."

When Acharya Shantideva told Yeshua, in the next review, that so far he had done very well and that he was now qualified to train as a monk, he was not enthusiastic. He told the Guru that he planned go back to his native Palestine, and reinterpret Judaism for his people. Guru Shantideva accepted this, but pointed out that the University regulations required that he complete seven years of study before he was declared a Scholar. Yeshua had completed only five years. How would he like to spend the remaining two years? Yeshua asked whether he could spend that time in the School of Medicine. This was rather unusual, thought Shantideva. But here was his best student, who had a very good cause. So he consulted the Acharya of the School of Medicine, and argued that healing was part of religion. After enquiring more about the candidate, the Acharya agreed to take Yeshua in, and assigned him to Physician Sanjeevan.

Sanjeevan had a detailed discussion with Yeshua about what he expected from the Medical School. "Medical course is normally of seven years' duration;

what can you do in one year?" asked Sanjeevan. Yeshua told his teacher what he wanted. He was going back to Palestine to do religious work. He wanted to include healing in his ministry. He would first like to know about the diseases which could be healed spiritually or by addressing the mind. The teacher explained that there were several psychosomatic diseases. "The problem is that it is often difficult distinguish them from physical ailments. For example, consider a person who cannot walk. It may be because there is a problem with his leg muscles or because he convinced himself that he could not walk. Another example is the case where the patient has lost his sensory perception. The complaint would be that he or she could not see, hear, or feel the touch. The cause could be a defect in the sensory organ - eye, ear, or skin, or the problem may have originated in the mind of the patient. The difference had to be evaluated by the physician through examination of the patient, his case history and by asking the right questions. There is a lot of subjectivity in this, and the right answers are found only by experience. The best way to learn was to go with the physician when he made the rounds of the ward".

This was exactly what Yeshua wanted. He accompanied Sanjeevan on his daily rounds of the ward and listened carefully to what the physician asked and what the patient answered. Later he would sit down and make notes. Sanjeevan was quite willing to discuss each case with Yeshua. The latter was impressed with the way the physician dealt with his patients. He quickly gained the confidence of the patients, with the result that they opened up to him. It was based on their responses to his questions and the medicines, that the line of treatment was decided. Unless it was an emergency or a serious illness, the initial medicine was generally Ayurvedic tonics. After the initial period when Yeshua was only an observer, Sanjeevan would ask Yeshua to give his evaluation of the cases. In other words, Yeshua was asked to decide which cases fell in the category organic problems in which the body had to be treated, and which cases were related to the mind where a psychological approach was called for. Gradually, the two of them developed consensus on this division. When the agreement became close, the teacher asked the student to take over the treatment of the latter group, where a spiritual and psychological approach was called for. However, there was one problem. The treatment involved putting the patient under hypnosis. Sanjeevan, therefore, taught Yeshua hypnotism. Quick learner that he was, Yeshua mastered this skill quite quickly. Sanjeevan now presented Yeshua to the patient, as well as his/her family, as a divine healer from Judea in Palestine, but explained to Yeshua that that he was doing this as it may help the healing process. With his beard and long hair Yeshua looked like a swami (Hindu Godman) and this helped. The next day, Yeshua went to a man, who was paralysed from waist down, and asked him: "Do you want to walk?" "Yes, Swamiji", replied the man. "Then rise up and walk" said Yeshua in an authoritative voice. The paralysed man walked out of the ward. "Miracle, miracle!" shouted the patients in the ward.

The next day another miracle happened. Yeshua asked his teacher whom he should attend to next. Sanjeevan pointed out the case of a blind man, whom both of them considered as a case for psychological treatment. Sanjeevan took out a small packet of Ayurvedic powder, and advised Yeshua to make it into a paste with water and apply it on the eyes of the blind man, and then ask him to wash it off. So Yeshua went to the blind man and asked him whether he wanted to see. When he got the affirmative answer, Yeshua applied the paste he was carrying on the eyes of the blind man. He then turned to the attendant of the patient and ordered: "Take him to the pond outside after a couple of hours and ask him to wash the medicine off, and he will see". After sometime the blind man came back running and shouting:"Now I can see, now I can see!". "Miracle, miracle", shouted all the onlookers in unison. After a few more miracles happened, Yeshua became a hero. He heard people whispering to each other: "Here is the divine Healer from Palestine. He can cure any disease." Some people followed him and requested him to visit their villages and cure their relatives.

Yeshua went to Sanjeevan and protested. "It is impossible for me to continue here. Everybody thinks I am some kind of a divine healer. But I know that is not true. You put me into this predicament. I have no option but to leave". "But you are not done yet. Your next lesson is in the psychiatric ward, which is very important to your mission" retorted Sanjeevan. "But people will chase me everywhere asking for miracles, which I cannot perform. I am just an ordinary guy. In fact, I cannot show my face anywhere", said Yeshua. "I have a solution for that. For some time, you work in another section of this school, where they teach Ayurveda. There nobody will recognise you. Ayurveda treats diseases with herbs and oils. It could be very useful in your mission", suggested Sanjeevan. "Later I will bring you into the psychiatric ward, which could have a major impact on your mission. Since outsiders are not allowed in there, you are unlikely to be recognised".

Yeshua saw the merit of this argument, and immediately reported to the Ayurvedic unit. There he was shown a large estate full of medicinal plants. Each variety was planted in rectangular plots, arranged in a regular grid with walkways and watering facilities. A guide rattled off the name of each plant and where it was used in treatment. However, these names did not register in Yeshua's mind. He was thinking how beautiful this garden was, and what a wonderful location it was for meditation, with a stream on one side and a mountain in the background. In spite of his lack of interest in the names of the plants, Yeshua noticed that they can be distinguished by the shape, size and colour of the leaves. Later he was taken to a large shed where medicines were prepared. Here the plants were crushed and the juice extracted and filtered. The resultant liquid was then processed by heating, evaporation, distillation etc. to the desired consistency (liquid, concentrate, ointment, paste, powder) before packing. Yeshua spent a few days studying the products and their applications in treating diseases. He realised that this was a specialisation in itself, requiring years of study. He noted down the names of a few powders and oils that he wanted to carry home with him.

One afternoon, Yeshua got a message that he had a visitor. He went to the reception area to find that the visitor was none other than Shakuntala. "How did you get here?" asked Yeshua. "I searched for you all over the School of Medicine and did not find you. At last I located you here" she replied. "There are several questions that the students asked in the Aramaic class, which I am unable to answer. You better come and clarify", "I am sorry that I missed my weekly appearance in your classes for the past few weeks. I am studying medicinal plants now" replied Yeshua and took his visitor to the Garden of Medicinal Plants. "At first, I had no clue as to what they were. Gradually I found that they could be distinguished by the colour, size and shape of the leaves. In each square plot of land that you see here, there is a placard announcing the name of the plant". "It is beautiful here" she said. "no wonder you have forgotten your commitment to the Aramaic class. You see that mountain over there in the south? That is the Margala Hills. We should go there on a picnic sometime. Meanwhile, please tell me when you will make your appearance in the Aramaic class. "I will come tomorrow", said Yeshua meekly. He mentally noted that Aramaic class was not the only reason she came here. "She obviously missed me", he thought and was quite pleased about it.

Yeshua then reported to his next station, namely the psychiatric ward. Psychiatric ward was isolated from the rest of the Medical School campus. It was also more secure, with guards checking all visitors. Only close relatives of patients were allowed to go inside. Most of the patients were admitted there because they themselves or their near relatives believed that they were possessed with demons. The symptoms were their abnormal or bizarre behaviour, as if they were controlled by someone else. Some suffered from convulsions, while others spoke in the voice and style of someone else. Violence and superhuman strength was often attributed to the patient. In some cases, the patient even gave out the name of the dead person who had taken 'possession' of him or her. As Yeshua was taken around the ward, Sanjeevan explained that he never believed in the idea of Demon Possession. One had to look for a psychological reason for the abnormality.

They stopped at the bed of a young woman who had a frightened look and was repeating the sentence: "He will kill me". Sanjeevan suggested that Yeshua should find some time to put her under hypnosis to find the cause of her fear, and then banish the evil spirit. The next day, Yeshua reported that the woman has been cured and can be discharged if Sanjeevan agreed. "Tell me what happened. What did you do?" asked Sanjeevan. Yeshua said:"First I enquired from her relatives about her background. It appears that her sister, who was close to her, died a few months ago after a fever. Our patient believes that her sister's husband killed her. The family thinks that she is possessed of her sister's ghost. I hypnotised her and got her version and told her that her sister died of fever. After I brought her back to normal state, I formally banished the ghost in the name of God Almighty. Now she looks OK". "You have many more ghosts to banish, young man", said the physician.

In the weeks that followed, Sanjeevan and Yeshua worked as a team, and studied many cases of demon possession. First they had to determine whether there was some organic problem or it was only a problem of the mind. Then they would interview the near relatives to find out when and how the current behaviour started, and whether there was any immediate cause such as a death or accident, which would have triggered the problem. Then they would carefully prepare for a session of hypnosis and choose the right questions to ask and make the right suggestions powerfully. Only after that the treatment would begin. The success rate was very high. The back logs in the ward slowly got cleared. New patients could be admitted for treatment. People started asking for the Jewish physician.

When Sanjeevan reported to the Acharya of the School of Medicine on the progress of Yeshua after a year in the School of Medicine, he expressed satisfaction. But he insisted that no medical education was complete without some knowledge of the physiology of human body. Therefore, Yeshua had to learn some physiology. Sanjeevan was happy with this development as he would be able to use Yeshua's talents in his wards. Yeshua agreed to accept the Acharya's decision without demur. So he started attending physiology classes, which he realised was important in any healing mission. As the course was practically designed for Yeshua, Sanjeevan had to play a crucial role in conducting and evaluating the short course. But he never complained as Yeshua was a very bright student who readily helped Sanjeevan in his work in the wards.

After he completed the medical part his course work, Yeshua was asked to meet Acharya Shantideva for his final verdict. Yeshua was asked to summarise his studies so far in Taxila. He recalled that he spent the first two and half years learning Pali. The next five years he spent in learning Buddhism and practicing Dharma. Then he spent one and a half year in the School of Medicine. The Guru went through his records, and said: "Your reports are all very good. But the minimum period stipulated by the University for this Course is seven years. Moreover, nowhere in your report it is stated that you have achieved Nirvana. So I propose that you continue your practice of Dharma until you experience Nirvana. All the others who complete this course become ordained monks and join the *Sangha*. Since you want to go back to your people, we will make an exception for you. You come back to me when you have achieved Nirvana or when you have completed six months of practice". At this point Yeshua had a question: "Guruji, I have the impression that *nirvana* is achieved at the end of ones life, except in the case of some saintly people. I have not yet completed thirty years. Do you think it is the right target for me?" Shantideva smiled and said: "It appears to me that your Course has not yet covered *nirvana*, which is the ultimate goal of our spiritual path. It can happen at the end of ones life when consciousness becomes free from the body. This is known as *nirvana* without remainder. When an ordinary person dies, his consciousness finds another body as host. In the case of *nirvana* after death, the consciousness is liberated and does not need a host. The happiness one feels on this liberation from *samsara* is beyond description. The *nirvana* that I am recommending to you is *nirvana* with remainder or *nirvana* in this life. It is achieved by following the eightfold noble path. *Nirvana* means extinguishing fires that cause suffering – fires of attachment [*raga*], hatred [*dvesha*] and ignorance [*avidya*]. If we get rid of greed, hatred and delusion, we can reach a state of perfect peace which is *nirvana* in this life." Yeshua asked: "Doesn't it mean that after one reaches *nirvana*, he will be treated as a saint and he will not be able to live a normal life? Shantideva answered by saying: "The state of *nirvana* does not mean withdrawal from normal life. People who have reached this stage are characterized by generosity, friendliness and wisdom. Their actions are not motivated by greed, hatred or delusion. Even after achieving *nirvana* you can discharge all your roles in society like practicing your profession, marrying, and raising children. However, in order to prevent slipping down to the previous level, you must continue your practice and regularly achieve *nirvana*. But I notice that you have a come a long on this path. I got reports that you have been regularly practicing the path even in the medical school. So it won't be difficult for you to come back in six months after achieving nirvana".

"The ultimate goal of all our practice of Dharma is permanent peace of mind which is what we achieve at *nirvana*. To reach this goal we have to practice renunciation. This can be reached only through training in five stages: 1. Affectionate love, 2. Cherishing love, 3. Wishing love, 4. Universal compassion and 5. Bodhichitta. Affectionate love helps us to develop a warm and friendly feeling to all living beings. It also helps us to get a balanced mind which is normally unbalanced on account of our preference for some and dislike of some others. The practice of affectionate love leads us towards cherishing love in which we cherish the welfare and happiness of all beings. This is achieved by equalising others with us and exchanging our position with those of others in a mental exercise. This practice teaches us that all others are as important as we are. The next step is wishing love in which we whole heartedly wish for the happiness and enlightenment of every living being. This takes us to the next logical step: universal compassion, which is the wish for the permanent liberation of all living beings from their sufferings. We should empathise with all of them, share their sufferings and meditate on this point. This is Bodhichitta. I hope you have noticed that a person who seeks his own peace of mind does not get enlightenment. The key to enlightenment is universal compassion or the sincere wish for the liberation of all Irving beings without exception".

Yeshua had another question. "Are Tanthric methods superior to the Sukta approach that you have taught us?" Shantideva shook his head and said: "Tanthric methods are controversial, mainly because they can be misused. I am not even sure that Buddha taught them. So we do not teach Tanthric methods in our course". As Yeshua had no more questions, the session ended with the renewal of Yeshua's commitment to come back after experiencing *nirvana*. He decided that he would come back only after both the conditions (*nirvana* and six months) were satisfied. It was only a matter of controlling the mind, and following the prescriptions given by various teachers who have already been there. Then there was Shakuntala to cheer him on. With relentless practice, Yeshua got there and the feeling was wonderful. Gradually, he could reach this state of ecstasy at the end of every meditation.

Yeshua reported back to Guru Shantideva only after six months, but the Guru was monitoring his progress through his own channels. Shantideva said: "Yeshua, I am glad to say that you have completed all the requirements for graduating from the School of Religion. Your graduation will take place along with other graduates in about a month. Meanwhile, I have a proposition to make. Though we call ourselves a School of Religion, we have been teaching only Buddhism, with some classes on Hinduism. You are our first graduate from a totally different religion. I propose that you join us as a temporary faculty member to start a course on comparative religion. As all the students are likely to be Buddhists, we don't need another teacher for Buddhism. I propose to invite Shakuntala to represent Hinduism, as she has done considerable studies on that subject. If you agree and continue the course for one or two years, then I feel that we may be able to manage it after that". Yeshua asked for a couple of days to think it over, and the Guru readily agreed.

Yeshua recalled that it was over ten years since he left his home and hearth. He was looking forward to going home and meeting his parents and siblings. The periodic messages brought by the caravan told him how anxious his family was to see him. Yohan was anxiously waiting for his return. At the same time, the unexpected offer he got was a once-in-a-lifetime opportunity. He had dreamt of such an opportunity to study different religions on a comparative basis. Further, Shakuntala will add value to the Course and lighten his burden. After much consideration he decided to accept the offer. Both Guru Shantideva and Shakuntala were happy with his decision. Yeshua was sanctioned a handsome remuneration for his new role. He decided to live modestly and save all the money he can, so that he did not have to depend on anybody when he got back to Palestine.

CHAPTER 4

Teaching Judaism in Taxila University

As soon as the course was announced, there was a rush for enrolment, ensuring its success. By agreement between the two teachers, Yeshua started the classes by teaching Judaism. He was surprised to find that the entire faculty of the School of Religion had also turned up along with the students to listen to him. He started with the biblical account of the story of creation. God created the heaven and the earth and all the flora and fauna in it in six days. When he started his work of creation, the earth was barren and empty. On the first day he created light to separate day and night. On the second day he created a vault called sky to separate the water above it from the water below. On the third day he separated the water below from dry land to form oceans. He created plants and trees of all kinds on the dry land. On the fourth day he created the sun and the moon and fixed them on the sky: the sun to rule over day and the moon to rule over night. They also controlled the seasons. On day five he created the fishes of the seas and the birds of the sky. On the sixth day, God created animals of all kinds. Finally he created man and put him in charge. Somebody raised his hand to ask a question, and the teacher signaled him to go ahead. "What is the authenticity of this story? Who witnessed these events?" Yeshua answered and said: "Obviously, no man could have witnessed these events, as man was created last. Moses may have written it down based oral traditions, or, as some people believe, got it as a revelation from God. Let me also point out that the picture of the universe that emerges from this story is rather primitive. One has to imagine a flat earth with a dome-like sky fixed over it. According to Ptolemy, the earth is round and the sun and moon rotate around it. In fact Eratosthenes estimated the circumference of the earth in an elegant experiment that he did. I will be happy to explain this experiment to those who are interested. He also measured the tilt in the earth's axis from its orbit as 23.5 degrees. This explains the change of seasons, which the biblical story cannot explain. We will examine later whether Moses actually wrote the Torah, which constitutes the first five books of Tanaka, the Jewish Scripture. Suffice it to note that the Torah asserts that God created the universe and everything in it". Most students wanted to hear about Eratosthenes's experiment; so Yeshua explained it in detail.

Yeshua continued: "Actually, I was planning to take this up at the end of the course, but on popular demand, I will explain it now. Eratosthenes was a Greek mathematician and astronomer who lived about two and a half centuries ago. He was from Cyrene, and was educated in Athens. The fact that he was selected and appointed as the librarian of the Alexandria library at the age of thirty by the Pharaoh himself shows how highly he was thought of. For Eratosthenes, it was a golden opportunity to have such a treasure house of books under his control, which he could read freely. He is best known for establishing a new subject called Geography. Coming to the circumference of the earth, Eratosthenes learned that on the summer solstice, when the day was the longest, sun would shine vertically overhead at noon in Syene, as seen from the fact that the sun's rays reach the bottom of a deep well without creating a shadow.. As a consequence, a straight stick driven into the earth vertically, like a stake, would have no shadow at noon at this place. On the other hand, in Alexandria, which was further north, a similar stake would give a shadow. Vertical stakes at these two places, when extrapolated downwards, should meet at the centre of the earth at an angle. The triangle formed by these two vertical lines and the surface of the earth is equivalent to the triangle formed by the vertical stake at Alexandria and its shadow. Please note that we ignore the small curvature of the earth between these two cities. Both are right angled triangles in which the second large angles are equal as they are on the opposite sides of two crossing lines. Therefore, by equivalence theorem, the acute angles are the same. By measuring the length of the stick above the earth and the length of its shadow, one gets a measure of the acute angle, which is the same as the angle subtended by the stakes at Syene and Alexandria at the centre of the earth. This angle was measured as one-fiftieth of the circumference of the earth by the experiment with the stick and its shadow at Alexandra. The arc of this angle on the surface of the earth was the distance from Alexandria and Syene, which was measured as 995 stadia. The circumference of the earth, which was found to be fifty times this, was therefore computed as 49,750 stadia. It is worth noting that all these deductions were easy for Eratosthenes because he learned Geometry from the land of Euclid and Pythagoras who invented the subject". A hand went up with a question: "How did he measure the tilt of the earth and how is it important?" Yeshua explained: "It is the tilt of the earth which gives us the seasons. If there was no tilt, we will have the same climate throughout the year. Because of the tilt, the Sun appears to travel north to give us summer and to the south to give us winter. In order to measure the tilt, we must remember that the sun is vertically above the equator on equinox when the day and night are of equal length. During the vernal [or spring] equinox, if you measure the angle of the shadow of a vertical stake at Syene, it right away gives the angle of the tilt as 23.5 degrees." Yeshua explained all this by means of diagrams drawn in sand.

The course turned out to be very popular because the Jewish teacher was proficient in current day knowledge in mathematics and science, was critically looking at his own religion, and permitted questions. Yeshua continued his narration by describing the creation of man. "The Lord God formed man out of the dust of the ground and breathed into his nostrils the breath of life; and he became a living being and was named Adam. God then planted a garden in Eden filled with all types of plants and trees. He also brought all the animals and birds into Eden, and asked Adam to name them. He put Adam in charge of all the flora and fauna. He then fashioned a woman out a rib of Adam to be a companion to him. In the centre of Eden there were two special trees - the tree of knowledge and the tree of life. Adam was forbidden to eat the fruits of these trees, but he was free to enjoy the fruits of all other trees. One day the serpent tempted Eve to eat the fruit of the tree of knowledge, saying that it would make her equal to God. She also gave it to Adam. With that, they could distinguish good and evil. They found themselves naked and used fig leaves to cover their nakedness. God got angry and banished Adam and Eve from Eden. He condemned them to hard toil all their lives so that they ate their food by the sweat of their brows, and limited their lives to 120 years. He cursed Eve and all women to difficult and painful childbirth."

"Adam and Eve gave birth to children. Their first son, Cain killed his younger brother Abel out of jealousy - the first case of murder. The killer was banished. Thus the line was continued through the third son, Seth. By the tenth generation, the earth was well populated. However, God was not pleased because of the wickedness of human beings. He decided to eliminate them from the face of the earth by means of a flood. However, he found a good man called Noah among the humans. God decided to continue the human race, as well as all the flora and fauna, by selectively saving a few. So he ordered Noah to build an ark. When it was finished, Noah was instructed to take on board samples of all species on earth in pairs, in addition to his own wife, his three sons and their wives. Then the sky opened and incessant rain pummeled the earth for forty days and forty nights. Flood waters rose and submerged all valleys and hills, and destroyed everything underneath. After the deluge stopped, it took several days for the water level to come down. At last Noah's ark set down on Mount Ararat. Life began all over again. Noah's sons Shem, Ham and Japheth became the progenitors of the great races that occupied Mesopotamia (Semitic people), Africa (Negroes) and North as well as East (Indo-Aryans). The population grew rapidly, and all of them spoke the same language. They developed the technology of brick making. They then got together and built a city with a tower that reached up to the sky. God got worried that these people were getting too powerful. So he created confusion among them by introducing many languages, breaking their mutual communication. He then scattered them all over the earth."

"The Great Flood was, however, a failure as it did not yield the intended result. Human beings continued their wicked ways. It appeared that sinful ways were built into them. Then God tried a different approach. God found a good man called Abraham. Unlike the people in his place of birth, he believed that there was only one god. For that he was persecuted by the King himself. He left his native Ur in Mesopotamia and moved to Canaan with his wife Sarah and brother's son Lot. Later he moved to Egypt in order to escape from a drought in Canaan. There the Pharaoh treated him well mainly because of his wife Sarah, whom he introduced as his sister. When the drought was over, the Pharaoh sent his guests back with lots of gifts. Abraham became very prosperous with a large flock of cattle and sheep, and scores of shepherds. Lot also became wealthy, and finally they decided to part ways in order to avoid conflicts."

"Clearly, God had chosen Abraham to be the patriarch of a new nation that he was planning. But there was a problem. Abraham had only one son and that from a slave girl called Hagar, but none from his wife. Here again God came to his rescue. Through divine intervention, the barren Sarah conceived, and thus a son was born to Sarah, whom Abraham called Isaac. In order to protect his succession, Abraham sent away Hagar and her son. Now God decided to test Abraham's obedience. He was asked to offer his only son in sacrifice to God on an altar built on top of Mount Moriah. Abraham obeyed without question. He went with Isaac to the top of the Hill, built an altar of stone, bound his son, placed him on the altar and raised his axe to strike, when God stopped him and showed him a wild goat to sacrifice. When Isaac grew up, Abraham found a bride for him from the house of Nabor, his brother. Rebekah and Isaac had two sons - Esau and Jacob. Esau became a hunter and was hirsute and smelled like an animal. Jacob was cunning and the favourite of his mother. He managed to become the successor of Isaac. It happened this way. One day Esau went hunting, while his brother stayed at home and made a pottage of red lentils. When Esau returned from his hunting trip, tired and hungry, he asked for a bowl of pottage from his brother. Jacob set a price for the lentil soup – Esau should transfer his seniority to the younger brother in exchange of a bowl of pottage. Esau was so hungry that he agreed to this condition. When Isaac was old and blind, Jacob managed to make this formal. His mother helped him to make his hands and neck hirsute by covering them with animal skin and to wear his brother's well-worn tunic. He then went and fed his father with the latter's favourite meat dish, cooked by Rebekah. Mistaking Jacob for Esau, Isaac blessed him and passed on all the rights of the first born to him. When Esau came home, he learned that he was cheated of his inheritance and got angry. Fearing the wrath of his brother, Jacob ran away to uncle Laban's place. There he wanted to marry Laban's younger daughter, Rachel. The price was seven years of service as a herdsman. But Laban cheated him and gave him Leah, the elder daughter on the wedding night. Jacob protested, and a compromise was reached; that Jacob could have the second daughter also, after another spell of seven years. Jacob continued to serve Laban even after the contracted fourteen years. Because of his effort, Laban became very prosperous. After a while, Jacob asked for a settlement of his wages based on the colour or spots of the animals. When this formula was accepted, he found ways of increasing the yield of the animals of his choice. Finally at the end of twenty years of service, Jacob fled, taking with him his family and his wealth."

"A hand went up and a young student was on his feet to ask a question. "The morality of the early Patriarchs is questionable. Abraham presented his wife to Pharaoh as his sister and became rich. Jacob conspired with his mother to fool his aged father into thinking he was the older brother and thus got the benefits due to the elder son. How can they be considered role models?" Yeshua said that he agreed with the questioner that the behaviors of these patriarchs were not ideal. "However, I suggest that these people should not be judged by the currently accepted standards of morality, but in the background of the world in which they lived."

Yeshua continued his narration: "When Jacob returned to Canaan, he was a wealthy man, with two wives, two handmaidens, eleven sons, a large herd of cattle, sheep and camels and scores of servants. All this he earned by working for his father-in-law Laban. In the process Laban also became very rich. Though he ran away from Laban, the latter caught up with him and they parted in peace. Now he had to make peace with his brother Esau, who was on his way with four hundred men. He selected a few of his best sheep, cattle and camels as a gift sent ahead of the main party, followed by his own animal wealth and then his family. He let them all cross River Jordan, and stayed back alone to contemplate on his impending encounter with his brother. Then he found himself wrestling with a stranger who could not defeat him. It turned out to be God himself. God blessed him, and renamed him Israel, the patriarch of a new nation. The next day he had a peaceful encounter with his brother, and proceeded to Bethel to thank God. As they neared Bethlehem, Rachel gave birth to a son and died. Thus Jacob had two sons from his favourite wife - Joseph and Benjamin. In all Jacob had 12 sons from his two wives and their handmaiden. They would become the patriarchs of the twelve tribes of Israel, known by the names of the patriarchs - Reuben, Simeon, Levi, Judah, Issachar, Dan, Naphtali, Gad, Asher, Joseph and Benjamin."

"Joseph and Benjamin, being sons of his favourite wife Rachel and the youngest, were particularly dear to Jacob. Thus these youngest two remained with Jacob when the older ones were sent to graze the cattle. The latter group was particularly jealous of Joseph, who received presents and praise from his father. One day, when the cattle grazers did not return as expected, Jacob sent

Joseph, now seventeen years old, to investigate. The brothers put Joseph into a dry well and later sold him to Ishmaelite traders going to Egypt with their wares. They then sold him to Potiphar, the chief of Pharaoh's palace guards, as a slave. Joseph proved to be competent and dependable, with the result that he gradually became the head of Potiphar's household operations. But he ended up in prison on the basis of a false charge by Potiphar's wife, because Joseph rebuffed her advances. In the prison he correctly interpreted the dreams of Pharaoh's butler and baker. When the butler was reinstated, he heard about Pharaoh's dreams, which nobody could interpret. At the butler's suggestion, Joseph was called. Pharaoh had actually seen two dreams. In the first one, he saw seven fat cows coming out of river Nile, followed by seven lean ones. The lean cows swallowed the fat cows. In the second dream, he saw seven fat ears of corn followed by seven shriveled ones. The latter group devoured the former. Joseph interpreted the dreams and explained that both of them have the same message. The next seven years will bring bumper harvests, but the seven years after that will bring very poor yields on account of severe drought. Joseph advised the Monarch that he should collect all the surplus grain of the first seven years, sell it to his people when the drought took hold. Pharaoh was pleased with the interpretation and the scheme, and put Joseph in charge of all the operations and gave him all the authority for implementation. This made Joseph the second most powerful man in the Empire."

"As the drought was widespread, it was felt in Canaan also. Jacob asked his elder sons to go to Egypt to buy grain. Without identifying himself, Joseph tried to find out about their father and younger brother. After some drama to keep the brothers on tender hooks, he identified himself and they had a great reunion. Pharaoh heard about it, and instructed Joseph to bring his father and the entire family to Egypt and settle them in Goshen which was close to Canaan. Thus seventy people including Jacob, his children, their wives, and grand children, along with their cattle as well as other movable wealth, settled in Goshen. They were assigned the choicest land to cultivate and to rear their animals. In course of time they multiplied and their prosperity also increased by leaps and bounds."

"In the first two years of drought, Egyptians bought grains from Pharaoh's bulging granaries against cash. Soon they ran out of cash. Joseph offered to sell them grain against gold and silver. When these were exhausted, they got grain against cattle. Later they were forced sell their land to Pharaoh, who then leased it to them against an assurance to give one-fifth of the yield to Pharaoh for all time. Only temple priests and Israelis were exempt. It was only natural that Egyptians hated Israelis, for they were jealous of the favours Pharaoh had shown them. They also realised that they lost all their possessions on account of the clever scheme that Joseph had devised. Jacob died at the age of 130, 17 years after settling down in Egypt. Joseph was the *de facto* ruler of Egypt until his death at the age of 110. His last surviving brother Levi, older by four years, outlived him by 23 years. After Levi's death there was no acknowledged leader of Israel, and it gradually lost its privileged position in Egypt. In a matter of three or four generations, new Pharaohs became hostile to Israel and Israelis became slaves. Then Moses arose as a giant of a leader."

"Moses grew up in Pharaoh's palace as the foster son of a princess. When he was born, his parents wanted to give him a better future than what they could afford. They made a floating baby basket out of reeds and left the baby in it among reed plants at the spot where the princes would come to bathe. His elder sister Miriam was asked to watch the baby from the cover of the foliage. The princess picked up the helpless baby, took him to the palace and brought him up. Obviously he had the best of everything - food, clothing and education in the royal palace. When he grew up, he realised that he was an Israeli, but his people were treated as slaves. He intervened in an argument between an Egyptian and a Hebrew, took the side of the Hebrew, and ended up killing the Egyptian. To escape the Pharaoh's wrath he ran away to Midian in the east. There he found favour with Jethro, a priest; and married his daughter Zipporah. While keeping Jethro's flock, he reached mount Horeb, where he had an encounter with God. God asked him to go back to Egypt and lead his people out of slavery into the promised land of Canaan. Moses protested and pointed out his deficiency in speech. God asked him to take his brother Aaron with him as he was a good speaker. 'But the Pharaoh is hardly likely to let my people go, if I just ask', protested Moses. God revealed his plan of using miracles to convince the Pharaoh. Thus Moses reluctantly went with Aaron and asked the Pharaoh to release the Hebrews so that they could go and worship their God in the wilderness. When he refused, Moses showed the first sign. He asked Aaron to drop his staff on the ground. It became a serpent. When Aaron picked it up by its tail, it regained its shape as a rod. But the Pharaoh was not impressed. Even his court magicians could do the same trick."

"When Moses reported his failure to God, he was told that the plan was to show several more miracles, which would be in the form of pestilence of increasing severity on the land and its people. God said that after each pestilence he would harden the heart of the Pharaoh so that he would refuse to let Israelis to go. Then God would send the next scourge, until the people could not bear it anymore. The whole process was planned for God's glory, so that Pharaoh knew that he was dealing with YHWH who is powerful. [YHWH is the name given for the God of Israel in old Hebrew which had no vowels. It may be pronounced as YaHWeH or YaHoWaH depending on the added vowels]. Thus the Egyptians saw their waters turning into blood, the scourge of frogs everywhere, all dust becoming lice, and swarms of flies all over the land. Now Pharaoh started to negotiate. He said they could worship in Egypt itself. Then he agreed to allow the men folk alone to go. Later he extended it to men and women, but the cattle had to be left behind. Meanwhile, more and miracles happened. The cattle of the Egyptians were slain one night, while sparing those of Hebrews. Ashes thrown up by Moses caused boils to appear on Egyptians. Hailstorm destroyed the entire vegetation like corn. Locusts covered the land, but when the Pharaoh relented, a strong west wind blew them away. Again he changed his mind, causing darkness everywhere for three days. Now God was ready with his last miracle. He asked the Hebrews to borrow gold and silver and other valuables from their neighbours, kill a lamb for each family and apply the blood on the front entrance. Then they were required to cook the lamb and eat it with unleavened bread. They should gird their loins and be prepared for a long journey with their families and possessions including cattle. At midnight the angel of God passed through the land and killed the first born son in each house, but spared the houses smeared with blood. The Pharaoh ordered all Hebrews to leave with all their possessions. Thus Hebrews started their march towards the Red Sea, en route to the Promised Land, from Ramses and Succoth. Avoiding the direct route, where they could end up fighting the Philistines, they veered South and camped at Etham on the edge of the desert. They then went along the coast and camped at Piha-hiroth, between the hill and the sea."

"But meanwhile, the Pharaoh changed his mind, and set out in hot pursuit at the head of an army column. When Hebrews reached Red Sea, God, operating through Moses, parted the waters and provided dry land for them to reach the other side. When Pharaoh's army was crossing the Red Sea, the water went back to their original position, drowning the pursuing army. There was much singing and dancing in the Israeli camp, led by Miriam, the elder sister of Moses.

After crossing the Red Sea, the Israaelis were led by God's angel towards the wilderness of Shur. They were guided by a pillar of cloud during the day, which turned into a pillar of fire at night. Soon problems surfaced of feeding a large population of men, women, children and animals, for which Moses had not made any preparation. In three days of trudging through the desert they ran out of water. Meanwhile, they had stopped near a pond of water called Marah, but its water was bitter. They started murmuring against Moses. All that Moses could do was to appeal to God. God showed him a tree whose branches, when dropped into the pond, could turn bitter water into sweet water. From Marah, God led them to the Oasis of Elim, where there were plenty of springs and palm trees. Then they were led through the wilderness of Sin towards Mount Sinai. Again people complained about food. They said that it was better to have stayed back in Egypt and eaten good food than to die of starvation in the wilderness. God told Moses that if the people agreed to obey his commandments, he would be willing to supply them food. In the morning he gave them Manna (honey bread) which covered the ground with the morning dew and in the evening he gave them meat, in the form of quail which covered the ground at that time. Slowly they moved towards Mount Sinai, all the time enjoying manna and quail meat. Now water became an issue once again. God asked Moses to take his rod and strike the big rock in front of him. Moses hesitated, but when he acted as ordered copious quantities of water came gushing out."

"Jethro, father-in-law of Moses, heard about the arrival of Hebrews at Sinai and came on a visit. He found Moses sitting all day long in the seat of judgment listening to disputes and giving judgment on behalf of God. Jethro pointed out that, if Moses did this single handedly for a population of over 600,000, he would soon wear out. He advised Moses to appoint men of character as judges over 1000 people. Each of them should have 10 judges who settle disputes over 100 people, and each of them should have 10 judges under them responsible for ten people. Thus smaller disputes would be resolved locally and those cases which were more difficult were referred to the next higher level. Only the most intractable cases would come to Moses. Moses gladly adopted this system. It was quite clear at this point that Laws have to be promulgated to form the basis of the decisions of judges."

"YHWH told that he would personally appear on Mount Sinai to convince the Israelis that he was their God who delivered them from Egypt and to make a covenant with them. Moses was asked to prepare the people through a process of purification for three days. On the third day YHWH would arrive on Mount Sinai (or Mount Horeb, where Moses first encountered God in a burning bush). Moses got the approach to the Mount barricaded so that the people would not come close to it, lest they die. Only Moses was allowed to go up the mountain to meet God. God's arrival was heralded by thick, black smoke emanating from the mountain. Moses explained to the people that God wanted to make a covenant with Israel. He explained the terms of the covenant, which meant that YHWH would be the only God they worship and Israel would follow all his laws. In turn YHWH would make Israel his chosen people and lead them to the promised land of Canaan. The people of Israel accepted these terms by acclamation. Moses then revealed the detailed plan that God gave him to carry forward the agreement. An Ark had to be built to locate the covenant. An altar and incense table of precise dimensions had to be built. These were to be located in a tabernacle of wooden posts and fine curtains. One set of the finest curtains would separate the holiest of holy place, where the Ark would be located and where YHWH would meet Moses, from the rest of the tabernacle. All these were to be made by the finest craftsmen of Israel."

"Moses stayed on the mountain for forty days, during which God made two stone tablets and wrote the Ten Commandments on them with his finger. When Moses came down the mountain with the two stone tablets under his arm, he saw his people worshipping a golden calf. Moses got so angry that he threw the stone tablets down and they broke. He went into a rage and attributed this disaster to the idolatry of his people. Moses took his tent of meeting and pitched it outside the camp. A column of smoke at the entrance to the tent announced to the people that YWHW had arrived at the tent to speak to Moses. He then asked those who were on the side of YHWH to come forward, to take swords in both hands, and kill all their brethren whom they find as they walked through the camp. 3000 Israelis were slaughtered in this operation. God, in his turn, sent a plague upon the people, which caused many more to perish. A great fear of God and his sole representative, Moses, spread through the camp. Moses then went up the mountain once again, this time with two tablets of stone. After forty days, he came back with the stones, with the commandments written on them. The Ark, the tabernacle with all the paraphernalia and courtyard were all set up as instructed by God and Aaron was consecrated as high priest."

"The covenant was the central piece in the tabernacle. It was in the form of two stone tablets on which the Ten Commandments were written, which was the basis of the Law that governed the life of all Israelis. The commandments were:

1. You shall have no other God but me (YHWH).
2. You shall not make any idols, nor worship any images.
3. You shall not take the name of the Lord, your God in vain.
4. Observe the Sabbath. Work for six days and keep the seventh day for rest.
5. Honour your father and your mother.
6. You shall not kill.
7. You shall not commit adultery
8. You shall not steal
9. You shall not bear false witness.
10. You shall not covet your neighbour's property, his wife or any of his possessions.

Moses himself elaborated on these laws, and gave supplementary explanations on their applicability to the human context. Gradually, specialists emerged who laid out all do's and dont's in the life of Israelis."

"As instructed by YHWH, Moses led Israel through the desert towards the Promised Land. A column of cloud representing God went ahead to guide them. It turned into a column of light at night. All along, Israel was fed manna and locusts. At last they reached Kadesh Barnea, where they set up camp. The promised land of Canaan was on the other side of the hills. Moses selected twelve strong men, representing the twelve tribes, to scout the land of Canaan. They reported back that the land was indeed fertile and the produce was good, but it was inhabited by people who were bigger and stronger who would be hard to defeat. Though Moses assured them that YWHW will go with them, the people were not confident. Joshua and Caleb were the only scouts who were positive about success with God's help. The diffidence of Israelis angered God, who asked Moses to return to the wilderness with a warning that none of the able-bodied men would see Canaan. So Israel wandered around the desert for thirty eight years more and returned to Kadesh Barnea. Thus they completed forty years after they left Egypt. By this time all the men who were afraid to go and possess Canaan were dead. God decided it was time for Israel to claim the Promised Land. They went around the land of Edomites, because they were refused passage through their territory, and peacefully passed through the areas occupied by Moabites and Ammonites, who were descendants of Abraham. When they came to Amorites, they killed King Shihon and his family, and then, as instructed by YHWH, slaughtered all the men, women and children, and occupied the land. Though the Promised Land was across Jordan River, it was decided to keep the land of the Amorites which was claimed by the tribes of Reuben and Gad. Moses agreed to this on the condition that they would also accommodate the half tribe of Manasseh, and that the able-bodied men would fight with the rest of the tribes until the whole of Canaan was conquered."

"Meanwhile Aaron died on Mount Hor as predetermined by YHWH and his son was ordained High Priest in his place. Moses had earned the wrath of YHWH in hesitating to coax the hard rock to yield water, and hence was denied permission to enter the Promised Land as punishment. But as a special concession he was allowed to get a glimpse of Canaan from Mount Nebo, where he died. Before his death, he nominated his close assistant and collaborator Joshua as his successor, to lead Israel to claim the Promised Land.

Joshua took over the leadership role, for which he was well prepared over the long years of close association with Moses. His first task was to cross River Jordan with the Israeli multitude. The tribes of Reuben, Gad and half of Manasseh were represented by their armies, as the women and children stayed back to tend their land. Joshua received ample guidance from YHWH, with whom he was in constant communication, as Moses himself was before his death. As instructed by YHWH, the priests carrying the Ark went first. When their feet touched the water, River Jordan stopped flowing, and the upstream water piled up like a wall. Israelis walked over the dry land to the other side. The last group to cross was the priests bearing the Ark. When they reached the other end, the river started flowing normally. Joshua's first target was the walled city of Jericho. For six days, he made the Israelis to march around the city walls, led by the trumpeters. On the seventh day the entire group shouted in unison, when prompted by the trumpets. The city walls went tumbling down. The Israeli army made mince meat of the surprised inhabitants, leaving no one behind. The next city they targeted was Ai. They had an initial setback there because of the sin of one man who kept some of the loot from Jericho for himself; but the campaign became successful after sinner was caught and punished with death for him and his family. Here Joshua adopted the tactic of luring out the defending army to chase part of the Israeli army, while the other part lying in ambush went and burned down the city, killing all men, women and children. People of Gibeon, another big city, managed to get a peace treaty with Israel by their representatives meeting Joshua and pretending to be from a far away land. When they were found out, Joshua made them menial labourers of Israel. Now the five Amorite Kings of Southern Palestine got together and mounted an attack on Gibeon, whose leaders then sent an urgent appeal to Joshua. He moved the entire army at his command over night to Gideon and surprised the Amorites. YHWH spread fear and confusion among the combined army, who started fleeing from the front. YHWH sent a hail storm which killed most of the attackers, and Joshua's army did a finishing job. The five kings were killed and buried in a cave."

"It took seven years to conquer the Southern Kingdoms of the Promised Land. Moses had already assigned the conquered territory east of Jordan River to the tribes of Reuben, Dan and half of Manasseh. The newly acquired lands on the right bank of Jordan were allotted to the tribes of Judah and Benjamin. The Tribe of Levi was not given a share like the other tribes, as they were on full time temple duty and entitled to partake of the sacrifices made to God. But they were given cities and pasture lands, so that they that they could feed their cattle. All this took seven years. Joshua felt that he was getting old. So without waiting for the rest of the Promised Land to be cleared of its inhabiting nations, he divided the land among the remaining seven tribes of Israel by taking lots. Each tribe was asked to occupy the allotted areas after eliminating the inhabitants with the help of the other tribes. However, this does not seem to have happened. In any case, the exising occupents were not fully eliminated.

Joshua died after allocating territories for the various tribes, without anointing a successor. This created a power vacuum, which was taken advantage of by strong neighbours. After twenty years of leaderless confusion, Cushan, King of Aram subdued Israel. The people repented and cried to YHWH for help. He relented and permitted the rise of a temporary leader named Othniel, a nephew of Caleb. This pattern of external oppression, repentance, and redemption continued for more than three centuries. The leaders who arose in this period became known as judges. Their leadership, character, extent of control (tribal or national) varied widely. Some like Gideon enforced the commandments. Some others were known for personal heroism, like Ehud who single handedly killed Eglon, the King of Moab, who was lording over Israel. Ehud was no model to the people - he was an illegitimate son of Gideon, who killed all the seventy legitimate sons. Samson, who acted as a one man army and performed hit and run operations against the Philistines, was not a model leader. In fact, he was caught by the Philistines in the house of a woman of ill repute. During the period of the Judges, Israel was under the oppressive rule of their enemies on five different occasions for a total period of 69 years."

"Samuel was the last of the Judges. He was also a prophet. Born to his mother when she was quite advanced in years, he was left with the Eli, the reigning Judge, at a tender age of two. Eli was tormented by repeated attack from Philistines. In the final battle, the Philistines won a convincing victory, killing Eli's sons and carrying away the Ark of the Covenant. Samuel was the logical successor to Eli and assumed charge at the age of thirty. His first task was to contain the Philistines. In consultation with YHWH, he asked Israel to assemble at a place called Mizpah. The Philistines watched the congregation with interest. When Samuel prayed for forgiveness of Israel's sins, YHWH sent an earthquake in the area where Philistines had taken position, killing most of them, and leaving the remainder in a state of shock. That was the end of Philistine problem for Samuel. His next task was to find a King for Israel. This was a popular demand of the people of Israel, because they found that the system of Judges was not satisfactory. First of all, there was generally a gap between the period one judge to the next, which led to anarchy or foreign domination. Secondly, the judges were not equally good or efficient. Continuity was lacking in the administration. Therefore, people appealed to Samuel to find a King and establish a monarchy as was the case with other nations. YHWH tried to dissuade the people by pointing out the deficiencies of a monarchical system. Once appointed, the King may turn out to be selfish and corrupt. There was no control over the King's succession, because it was by hereditary. The successor may turn out to be worse than his predecessor."

"But the people were adamant in their demand, and hence God chose Saul of the tribe of Benjamin as the first King of Israel. One of his qualifications was that he stood head and shoulders above the others. As instructed by YHWH, Samuel anointed him King of Israel. Samuel then called for a conclave of

Israel at Mizpah. He showed how God selected Saul. When Saul was found and brought in front of the conclave, he stood taller than everybody else. The people of Israel accepted him as their King, though some demurred. Saul got his opportunity to prove himself in his new role when the Ammonites threatened to attack an Israeli city. He gathered an army of three hundred and thirty thousand men from all the tribes of Israel, and mounted a surprise attack on the Ammonites, practically finishing them off. This convinced all of Israel of Saul's royal stature. Now Samuel called all Israel to Gilgal and, in the presence of the Lord, crowned Saul as King of Israel. Later, Saul was asked to finish off the Amalekites, killing not only all the people, but also all their cattle. Saul succeeded in this mission, but let the king live and allowed the troops to keep the fruits of battle including the cattle and other animals. Because of this disobedience Saul lost favour with the Lord, who decided to replace him. The choice fell on David, the eighth son of Jesse, a wealthy man from the tribe of Judah. David was often in the fields keeping sheep, but he was also a harpist. Samuel was ordered to anoint him with oil. As the spirit of the Lord left Saul, he started feeling depressed. David was brought to play the harp to cheer him up and Saul made him a member of his staff."

"Meanwhile, the Philistines amassed a huge army to fight Israel. Saul also marshaled his army. A Philistine giant named Goliath strutted about challenging Israelis to send one man for combat with him to decide the fate of the war. The frightened Israeli soldiers went into hiding to avoid a fight with the giant. Young David, armed with only his sling and stones, went to battle Goliath, who laughed at the foolhardy boy. But David sent a projectile from his sling in the name of YHWH, and hit Goliath on his forehead, with result the giant collapsed. Now David cut the giant's head with the latter's sword and took it with him as trophy. The Philistines ran away in panic. Thus David became the hero of Israel. Recognising the potential threat from David, King Saul tried to kill him. Meanwhile the Philistines regrouped and mounted an attack on Israel. In the ensuing battle Saul's sons were killed, and the King was mortally wounded. Saul died of his own sword, by falling on the pointed instrument. Meanwhile, David formed an army and won a great victory over Amalekites. He distributed the spoils among his allies, and sent some to the elders of Judah, who anointed him King of Judah. In the North, Saul's fourth son Ish-Bosheth was crowned King in place of his father. But he did not last long. He was murdered after two years of reign. David now became the King of all of Israel, and ruled for thirty years. David became a popular king, as Israel was happy with his military exploits especially against the Philistines, his wise rule, and the psalms he wrote to praise YHWH. But the Lord did not permit him to build the Temple in Jerusalem. Instead David built his palaces and married scores of young women. He also earned some bad points for his sexual escapades. The most notable was the use of his royal position to bring to his bed Bathsheba, the beautiful wife of Uriah, a Hittite military officer. Later he got Uriah killed on the battle front. Bathsheba became his favourite queen, and manipulated David with her charm to make her son the successor, overlooking the claim of his eldest son. Before Solomon's succession, his two elder brothers had revolted against David. First Absalom started a civil war, which David managed put down with the help of loyal troops. When he was dying, another son Adonijah crowned himself King. By the timely intervention of Bathsheba, her son Solomon succeeded David."

"Solomon was very young when he ascended the throne. In the fourth year of his reign he started the construction of the Temple in Jerusalem, which was long-felt need of Israel. The Temple was completed in seven years. Then he started building his opulent palaces. He is not credited with any major military victory, but said to have accumulated a lot of wealth, most of it through heavy taxation. He had 700 wives and 300 concubines. Most of them were of non-Israeli origin, to please whom Solomon set up altars for their deities and made sacrifices there. Obviously, this did not please YHWH, who decided to punish Israel after the death of Solomon. During his long reign, Solomon appears to have ensured peace with powerful neighbours by paying them off through tributes.

After Solomon's death, his son Rehoboam succeeded him. The new King announced to his subjects, who were already groaning under heavy taxation, that he would increase the taxes as well as punishment. Jeroboam, who is described as a servant of Solomon, led the revolt, and became the king of the ten northern tribes, leaving Rehoboam with only two tribes. Thus the Northern Kingdom started off with a king with no royal blood in him. Further he discouraged the periodic journey of Israelites to the Temple in Jerusalem and encouraged the worship of gods other than YHWH. These actions did not find favour with YHWH. Out of the twenty kings of the Northern Kingdom, fourteen died unnatural deaths. They were murdered or met a violent end. The successor always ensured that all the progeny of the predecessor were annihilated, obviously to prevent the rise of a competitor. This was in fact the general practice in those days. After David became king, Saul's progeny disappeared from the face of the earth. After Solomon's ascension to the throne no other heir survived. So it was with all the kings of Israel. The Capital of the Northern Kingdom was Tirzah until Omri built a new capital called Samaria. Omri also started the Omride dynasty. Ahab, son of Omri had many military victories to his credit. But the Kings of Samaria cannot be compared with the powerful nations of that time, whether it is Aram (Syria), Assyria, Egypt or Babylon. Samaria survived as a vassal state of Assyria. Assyrian King Tiglath-Pilesar III made Hosea a vassal king. His son Shalmanesar V found out that Hosea was not paying royalty to Assyria but to Egypt. So he laid siege to Samaria, and ransacked it. It was his son Sennacherib who captured the city and deported the inhabitants to other parts of the Kingdom, and replaced them with his subjects from other areas. This happened about seven centuries before our time. Thus ended the story of the Northern Kingdom which lasted for about two and a half centuries."

"The Southern Kingdom of Judea lasted for a little over a century more. They were the real descendants of David and Solomon, with royal blood in their veins. But blood-letting, even of the royal variety, was not uncommon. The kings came in many hues. Some like Ahaz or Manasseh did not follow the commandments, especially those relating to worshipping YHWH exclusively. Some like Uzziah, Hezekiah and Josiah followed the Laws of YHWH, and even enforced them. Josiah is particularly noteworthy. Unlike his father Manasseh, he was steadfast in his loyalty to YHWH. He cleaned the Temple and found a scroll with laws of the Lord written on it. It could be a part of the book of Deuteronomy. Deeply moved by the prospect of doom that may fall on Judea, he called all the elders, and together they made a covenant with YHWH to follow his commandments. He destroyed all the shrines and equipment used to make sacrifices to other Gods, and killed the priests who performed these rites. About this time, Neco the Egyptian Pharaoh was moving north with his army to help the Assyrian King. Josiah, with his army tried to stop Neco. An arrow from a sharp shooter hit Josiah and he died a painful death. Meanwhile, the Assyrian Kingdom collapsed, and Babylon, under Nabopalasser, became the most powerful Kingdom in the region. His son Nebuchadnezzar attacked Jerusalem, and extracted a heavy ransom from Judea. The invaders took all the valuable treasures of Jerusalem, including all the gold and silver. They also took 100,000 of the best and the brightest of the population and marched them to Babylon. The Babylonian army returned a few years later and besieged Jerusalem, because the puppet king Zedekiah was not paying the promised tribute. When food ran out, the king and the noblemen escaped through a hole in the wall, but they were caught and taken prisoners. The Babylonians then razed the Temple, tore down the walls of the city and took away anything worthwhile such as bronze articles, utensils etc. All except the very poor were taken to Babylon. Thus the end of the Southern Kingdom came about 600 years before our time."

"The Babylonian sojourn was not an unpleasant experience for the captives. The bright ones were given training and given Government jobs, and the craftsmen could easily find work. Some bright people, like Daniel, rose to high positions. Babylon was a lot more prosperous than Judea and the land was fertile, with plenty of water. The captives lived in relative freedom, unhindered by Jewish priests who restricted their lives back in Judea. The Babylonian Empire was set up through the efforts of Nabopolassar. His son Nebuchadnezzar expanded it through cruel cunning and outstanding military strategy. At its peak, it spread from Persia to the Mediterranean, and even Egypt. However, it disappeared faster than it sprang up, just a couple of decades after the death of Nebuchadnezzar. The last King was Belshazzar. He hosted a drinking party for the noblemen of Babylon. They drank from the golden vessels lifted from the Temple of Jerusalem. At this time Cyrus, King of Persia besieged Babylon, whose walls were almost impregnable. The Persians diverted River Euphrates, which was flowing under the city, and marched in through the dry river bed. It is said that the people of Babylon were so fed up with their king that they welcomed the invaders. Cyrus thus smoothly took over the city, and with it came an empire. It was all over for the Babylonian Empire in less than a century."

"The Persian Rulers of the Achaemenid Dynasty were more civilized than their predecessors. Cyrus the Great, in his first year of rule, issued a decree permitting Jews to return to Jerusalem and to rebuild the temple. Thus 42,360 men trudged back home with their wives, children, animals and other possessions, under the leadership of Prophet Ezra. They rebuilt the altar and made a sacrifice on it. But they could not proceed further because of local opposition. It was Darius I, the third king of the Achaemenid Empire, who ordered the construction of the Temple at the expense of the State. He was evidently influenced by his Jewish wife Esther to take this step. In the sixth year of the reign of Darius, the Temple project was completed. It took several years more for the walls of the city to be completed. Eventually the Persian (Achaemenid) Empire gave way to Alexander the Great, who built up the largest empire the world had seen, stretching as it did from India in the east to Egypt in the west. The Greeks also gave the world an excellent language of communication, along with its literature, mathematics and science, and a system of libraries. After Alexander's premature death, his four generals divided the empire among themselves. Ptolemy got Egypt, but enlarged his share by annexing Palestine. His successor Ptolemy II noticed that there was no Jewish scripture in the library, because the Jewish priests were not willing to give their sacred manuscripts to the library. So he made a deal with the priests and purchased the right for translation. Thus a Greek version of the Torah called Septuagint was born. This made the Torah accessible to all Greek speaking people."

"Eventually the Greek Empire collapsed, and Romans became the super power. They needed the help of Antipeter to fight the Parthians. This resulted in his son Herod (the Great) becoming the king of Palestine. But he was not a Jew, but an Edumian. He started the reconstruction of the Temple, but died without completing this project. This happned only a quarter of a century before our time. His son Herod Antipas I became the king of Galilee and Perea, while Judea together with Samaria was directly ruled by Rome through a Prefect called Valerius Gratus."

"Yeshua concluded his presentation by saying that he went through the entire history of the Jews because Judaism was inextricably linked with their history. The historical narration in the Torah started with the story of creation in which God created man in his own image. But the first couple disobeyed God and had to be sent out of the Garden of Eden. Disgusted with the continued disobedience of human beings, God decided to create a great flood to wipe up out the whole of mankind. But he relented and allowed one family - that of Noah - to survive. Later YHWH led Abraham from his polytheist hometown to monotheism in Canaan. His grandson Jacob was named Israel and anointed as the father of a great nation. Jacob, along with his children and grandchildren, had to move to Egypt to escape from famine. But they multiplied fast into a nation. YHWH now sent Moses to liberate Israel from Egypt, and take them to Canaan. Along the way he gave them the Ten Commandments on two stone tablets. Later, Moses gave detailed regulations that govern the life of each Israeli, which he claimed to have received from YHWH. Israelites were led into the Promised Land by Joshua, Moses' successor who was guided by YHWH. Joshua exterminated some of the native tribes and divided the land among the twelve tribes of Israel. In the next phase, Israel was led by Judges who arose sporadically. Then YHWH gave them kings like David and Solomon. After that the kingdom was split into two, with the larger fraction going to Jeroboam, a commoner, who became the king of the northern kingdom. Only two tribes remained with Solomon's son. The Northern Kingdom ended when Sennacherib ransacked the capital and deported Israelis to other parts of the Empire. The end of Judea came when the Babylonian King Nebuchadnezzar attacked Jerusalem and took the Jews as prisoners to Babylon. The Persian (Achaemenid) kings allowed the Jews to return to Jerusalem to rebuild the Temple. The Persians were followed by Greeks and later by the Romans. Now, Judea is ruled by Valerius Gratus, the Roman Prefect."

In summary, Yeshua said: "The Jews are expected to conduct themselves by the Law of Moses. The Law itself is a big compendium regulating human behaviour in various situations. As new situations arise, the Rabbis give their interpretations of the law to cover such cases. This has made the Law a big legal document, and we have to approach a Rabbi to find out how to behave. It is the job of the priests to enforce the Law and punish those who do not conform. This makes the priests very powerful. Briefly stated, Judaism is the acceptance and worship of YHWH as the only God, and obedience of his commandments as given in the Law of Moses. Tanaka is the Jewish Scripture, which shows how YHWH intervened in human history to enforce his laws and to help his chosen people in their times of trouble. The prophets and the psalms tell us that God is compassionate and listens to our prayers. Let me end up by reciting a beautiful psalm that David wrote, drawing an analogy from his shepherd days. As I recite it, it will be obvious why Jews often sing this psalm, particularly in times of trouble.

The LORD is my shepherd, I lack nothing.
　He makes me lie down in green pastures,
he leads me beside quiet waters,
　　he refreshes my soul.

He guides me along the right paths
    for his name's sake.
Even though I walk
    through the darkest valley,
I will fear no evil,
    for you are with me;
your rod and your staff,
    they comfort me.
You prepare a table before me
    in the presence of my enemies.
You anoint my head with oil;
    my cup overflows.
Surely your goodness and love will follow me
    all the days of my life,
and I will dwell in the house of the LORD
    forever

DISCUSSIONS

Though Yeshua encouraged questions in his classes, it was the discussions at the end of the course that turned out to be the most exciting. Yeshua allowed his audience to ask all the questions they had, and classified them into groups. The first group of questions related to the authenticity of the Scripture, its authorship, the language in which it was written, whether any of the original texts were available, in what manner they were preserved etc.

Yeshua pointed out that the answer depends on who gives it. "A believer Jew would say that the Torah was written by Moses, as dictated by YHWH. According to the Torah, the Ten Commandments were written on stone tablets by the Lord himself. If the purpose of writing was to communicate with the people, then the writing must be in a language that the people understand. The only language for writing at the time Moses lived was Cuneiform, featuring wedge shaped symbols scored on clay tablets with reeds, which were then baked for preservation. It is difficult to communicate the ideas in the Torah using this language. Even if someone attempted it, he would need far too many tablets to be practical. One has to assume that the scripture was orally handed down from generation to generation. The problem with this kind of transmission is that the text gets modified along the way."

"The question, therefore, is this: when did written language develop sufficiently to have the capability to record complex and abstract ideas. This required a syllabic language in which a limited number of alphabets could produce a large number of syllables, which could be strung together to make a very large number of words. A beginning towards this was made by Phoenicians. One can see a further development in old Hebrew where 22 consonants were used to make words, but there were no vowels. This made it difficult to understand these texts, which appeared over six centuries ago. The newer Hebrew and Aramaic, which came later, provided better platforms for writing. It is believed that Hebrew Scriptures were written during the Babylonian sojourn. That is consistent with the development of written language. In fact, it is possible that the writing of the Torah started in Babylon and was completed in the rebuilt Jerusalem. This also conforms to the claim of the Rabbis that Tanaka was adopted some three or four centuries ago."

"The strength of a language is in its literature. The first language that built up a strong written literature was Greek. Homer's epics like Odyssey and Iliad may have been in oral form at first, but written later in alphabetic Greek. The Greek culture could boast of great mathematicians like Pythagoras and Euclid, scientists like Archimedes, and Philosophers-cum-teachers like Socrates, Aristotle and Plato. The Greeks also built libraries that made this knowledge accessible to the people. Septuagint is a book in Greek that popularised the Torah. In fact, Septuagint became an authentic sourcebook. To come back to the basic question of authenticity, most of the Scriptures were oral traditions, which were written down only fairly recently. The events described were not witnessed by the authors."

The second set of questions related to the nature of God, his character and the nature of his interaction with humans. For example, if God spoke to Adam or Abraham, in which language did he speak? Later, he appears to have reduced this type of interaction. During exodus, he spoke exclusively to Moses, and then to Joshua. Later the Prophets spoke for him. Now he seems to have stopped his one-to-one interaction altogether. Similarly, miracles seem to have dried up, but earlier it was a daily affair. For example, during exodus and in the battles in Canaan, YHWH won many battles for Israel by sending hailstorms, earthquakes, pestilence etc, or by parting the red sea or River Jordan. The question is whether such conversations or miracles really happened, and if they did, why don't we see them today?

Yeshua answered this by pointing out that earlier the story the more likely it was described as a miracle. For example, eclipses are now understood to be natural phenomena, but earlier they were thought to be foreboding evil. Thus we see a gradual increase in the understanding of natural phenomena and a corresponding decrease in miracles. Yeshua said that all these questions had one answer. The Scripture was not written by God, but by human beings. The authors of the written texts never witnessed the events they described. They took the current version of the orally transmitted stories. There is a great advantage in writing prophesies long after the event. Prophesy can be made exact.

Regarding the nature of God, the main question was on the cruelty of YHWH, who ordered the killing of innocent Canaanites, just to give their land to Israelis. Another example of this cruelty was seen in the butchering of animals to provide burnt offering to please God. YHWH was also not impartial in his reward and punishment system. He did not punish David for killing a Hittite military official for the purpose of marrying his wife or his son Solomon who worshiped other gods along with multifarious wives. But both David's predecessor and Solomon's successor were punished for lower offences.

Yeshua began his answer by saying: "There is only one God, and, in my opinion, he treats all people the same way, as they are all his children. His rules are applicable to all humanity. The problem is that different groups have their own gods, and they expect to get favourable treatment from them. Jews believe that they are the chosen people of their god YHWH. This has done a lot of good to their self-confidence and helped them to survive for a long time in hostile environments. But if this confidence leads to ill treatment of their neighbours, it will not be acceptable to God Almighty. The statement that God created man in his image was written to convey the meaning that we should strive to be like him in our character. The converse is not true. God is not limited by our physical features and limitations. I am limited by my body which cannot survive for even a few minutes without air, even a few hours without water and not more than a few days without food. If I am here, then I cannot be elsewhere at the same time. If God has the limitations of a human body, he cannot be omnipresent, omnipotent and omniscient."

When somebody states that God spoke to him, it means that he felt that God spoke to him. A more rational way of saying it is that this is how I think God wants me to act. Or this is the action that befits God's laws or his character. Coming to the specific questions, Israel believes that YHWH was with them when they won their battles. When they lost, it was punishment for disobedience. David and Solomon were the greatest kings in their whole history, and so their chroniclers are quite forgiving to them, but I wonder whether God would be equally forgiving. I do not think God would sanction large scale killing of people, and for that matter the slaughter of animals to make burnt offerings to him. Let us not blame God for the evil that men do."

The third set of questions related to God's hand in history. One questioner put it very bluntly. If YHWH wanted to develop one nation as his special people, he has failed in his mission. He created Adam and Eve in his own image, but ended up driving them out of the Garden of Eden. When they multiplied and inhabited the earth, God sent the great flood to destroy his creations. Then he relented and let one family survive along with one pair of each species. Then he started developing Abraham and his family. He used Moses to liberate them from Egypt. Moses gave them the Law, but they did not obey him. He gave them kings, but that experiment was not successful. Assyrians finished off ten tribes, and the rest were taken captive by Babylonians. Now the remnant is ruled by Romans. Doesn't it show that YHWH has failed? Another questioner asked: Why does YHWH want to be praised and worshipped all the time? Isn't such vanity a human weakness?

Yeshua answered by saying: "You are criticising the writers of the Scripture and not God. Yes, the Israeli chroniclers have said that YHWH wanted burnt offerings to be made to him and that he wants to be worshipped. That is their interpretation of Israeli history. Who failed? Israel or God? Is it right to say that YHWH used Babylonians to punish Israel? Why are Babylonians worthy of help from YHWH even to punish Israel? Alternatively, one can say that because Babylonians were successful, the chronicler says that they were used to punish Israel."

One question was on the Jewish concept of heaven. Yeshua said that all the religions on earth describe heaven as the abode of God and that is located high up in the sky. According to Tanaka, only two people went directly to heaven without dying. They were Enoch, an ancestor of Noah, and Elijah, the prophet. Is this a believable story? Hardly! If a human being goes up in the sky, he encounters lower and lower atmospheric pressure. First, he will gasp for breath in the rarified atmosphere and blood will start coming out of his nostrils first, and other organs later. It is clear that the author of the stories did not know much about the body nor about atmospheric pressure. It was interesting, he said, that in all religions heaven is considered the abode of gods, located up there somewhere. It may be related to the idea that higher is superior, so that we want go up rather than down.

One scholar stood up and said: "Sir, the emphasis that you place on education and knowledge is obvious. It was clearly visible when you explained the experiments of Eratosthenes, Are there similar anecdotes from Jewish history? Were the Jewish leaders educated?" Yeshua replied: "There is no mention in Tanaka about education. Israelis were slaves in Egypt and hence they were unlikely to have received any education there. Of course, Moses grew up in Pharaoh's palace and therefore he would have got his education there. But there is no mention of a general education system. We know that some Rabbis conduct classes in the Scripture for those preparing for priesthood. But there is no indication of a general education system." The questioner persisted: "Is that the reason why Jews have not contributed much towards human knowledge as the Greeks have done, through advances in mathematics, science, geography and philosophy?" Yeshua answered and said: "You may be right on that point. We know that nations possessing better educational systems make more seminal contributions. I would say that a written language that aids in disseminating knowledge plays a key role. Let me also add that too strict an adherence to a religious order and its enforcement by priests inhibits free thinking and, therefore, is detrimental to progress. Another scholar interjected: "Sir, don't forget that Socrates was killed by poisoning, by the very people you are praising." Yeshua: "Anybody who advocates change runs the risk of persecution by the champions of *status quo*. Please remember that by his death, Socrates furthered the cause of freedom of speech." The original questioner was on his feet again. He said: "Sir, I am fully satisfied with your reply. I salute your courage in critically looking at your own religion." The entire audience burst into applause.

Shakuntala asked whether she could ask a question. "Of course, you can. It will be my pleasure to attempt to answer your question" said Yeshua. Shakuntala: "You told me that you want to go back to Palestine to reinterpret Jewish Laws. What is the nature of modification to the Scriptue that you would suggest?" Yeshua: "Fortunately, I have thought about it and therefore I can readily answer your question. In my opinion, the problem with Judaism is that it is old and ritualistic and not very amenable to change. The Law of Moses was a great improvement over the contemporary practices. But it needs improvement based on our more recent experience. For example, the Ten Commandments sought to regulate interpersonal relationships by forbidding killing, stealing, bearing false witness, and coveting the neighbour's property. Observances of these laws were enforced by the priests. I would like to move this responsibility to individuals, so that they can review their actions and their consequences. In place of prohibitions, I would suggest a proactive approach. For this purpose, I would stress love rather than hatred, forgiveness rather than revenge and reconciliation rather than litigation. I believe this will bring more social harmony. I would propose that we should stop looking at others as adversaries, but consider them as brethren." Shakuntala applauded him and added one more point. "It appears to me that your laws are male-centric. It would be good if you can take into account the fact that women exist in equal numbers as men. It is unfortunate that they are treated as an expendable commodity." Yeshua replied: "I agree with you. But please remember that this is not the problem with Jews alone. All societies are patriarchal and women are treated as junior partners. This is obviously based on the perception that women are the weaker gender and need to be protected. It will take a lot of effort to change this. All I can say is that I will treat women with respect." "I am sure you will" said Shakuntala. "But for your fairness, I would not have been a partner in conducting this course". After ensuring that there were no more questions, Yeshua declared that the course on Judaism was completed and that Shakuntala would give the next course on Hinduism. The whole audience stood up and gave him a standing ovation.

CHAPTER 5

A Course in Hinduism

Shakuntala now led the discussion on Hinduism. In her preface she wondered whether she could really be called a Hindu. She was born in a Hindu family and remembers to have gone to temples with her mother, but after her father moved to Taxila, there was more Buddhism discussed at home than Hinduism. This had given her an advantage: She could look at Hinduism dispassionately. As she studied the religion, she found it fascinating. In this study she had a major handicap: there were no written documents to go by.

"Hindu Scriptures are very old, dating back to the Vedic period which began in the bronze age and extended up to about 500 years before our time. The Scriptures consist of four Vedas - Rig Veda, Sama Veda, Yajur Veda and Atharva Veda - and the two epics: Ramayana and Mahabharata. They are believed to have been composed by great *Rishis* (Sages) many centuries ago, and orally transmitted from generation to generation. They were composed in Sanskrit, considered to be the oldest language. However, Sanskrit does not have a script for writing. Therefore, only the oral versions are available. There have been suggestions to write the sacred text in *Brahmi*, the script found on Asoka's *Stupas*, but there has not been much progress in that direction. Critics will say that oral versions cannot be authentic, as the texts could get modified in the process of transmission. Believers counter it by pointing out that the oral texts have a well defined meter and rhythm, with structured enunciation providing inflections and permutations, which protect the texts against corruption. However, it is also possible that later Sages could make additions and subtractions, while retaining the meter and the rhythm. I am saying all this at the beginning so that I don't get questioned about authenticity. I am not as smart as Yeshua in handling questions", she said. *You are not only smart, but also beautiful,* thought Jeshua.

All this meant, she continued, that she had to brush up her Sanskrit and listen to the recitations of two different schools. It was indeed a rewarding experience. She then proceeded to describe Rig Veda, the oldest and the most important *Veda*. "Rig Veda is a collection (*samhitha*) of hymns (*suktas*) consisting of 1017 hymns in 10,600 stanzas. It is divided into 10 Mandalas (books). Mandala 1 has 191 hymns addressed to Agni, the fire god. In fact Rig Veda opens with the word Agni. Mandala 2 contains 48 hymns addressed to Agni and Indra, the Lord of the Sky. Mandala 3 consists of 62 hymns to Agni, Indra and *Vishvedevas* (universal deities). This book contains Gayatri *Manthra,* whispered in the ears of new Brahmin initiates. Mandala 4 has 58 hymns addressed to Indra and Agni. Mandala 5 consists of 87 hymns, mainly addressed to Agni and Indra and some to *Vishvedevas.*(universal deities). Mandala 6 contains 75 hymns addressed to Agni, Indra and others. Mandala 7 comprises 104 hymns addressed to the same deities as above. Mandala 8 has 103 hymns to Varuna, god of water. Mandala 9 is recited at *Soma Pavamana,* a ritual of purification of Soma, a somewhat intoxicating drink with curative powers. Mandala 10 consists of 191 hymns to Agni, Indra and others. It also includes *nadi stuthi sukta* describing rivers and thus giving a clue to the location of these people, namely those who composed and used this part of the *vedas.* In fact, from this *sukta* we know that the rivers in their country were flowing from north to south, suggesting that the Greater Punjab as their location".

"*Sama* Veda, the second Veda, is a collection of hymns drawn from Rig Veda but set to musical notes so that they can be sung. There are no additional lessons to be learned from this Veda and it will not be considered further. *Yajur* Veda is a collection of *manthras* that can be used by priests on ceremonial occasions, essentially taken from Rig Veda. The officiating priest mutters the *manthras* while making sacrificial offerings. Thus *Yajur* Veda is essentially a book of rituals. The fourth Veda, Atharva Veda, is the longest of the four and different from others. It focuses on ritualistic prayers and sacrifices to meet the needs of individuals as well as the society. Thus there are charms to cure diseases and possessions by demons of disease. Some of the *manthras* are for cure from fever, cough, jaundice, constipation, diarrhea, and colic pain. There are oblations to the sun to cure paralysis. There are *manthras* for cure from leprosy, healing of wounds, as well as against poison including snake poison. There are charms to promote growth of hair, to increase virility, and to drive out demons. There are chants for ceremonial wearing of amulets against diseases and demons which cause diseases. There are hymns of praise of medicinal plants used in the treatment of diseases and injuries. There are charms against all diseases, and for long life as well as for perfect health. Charms are also available to repel sorcerers or spells, to obtain a husband, wife, or son, to win the love - even passionate love - of a member of the opposite sex. *Atharva* Veda also contains prayers made at ceremonial occasions like the coronation of a king and for the lustre, power and glory of the king. There are charms for victory in battle and also prayers for harmony. Home building and agriculture are not forgotten. Charms against the danger of fire were for everone, but shepherds sought protection from wild beasts and robbers. Some wanted success in gambling, while others wanted protection from calamity. There are hymns for invoking Sun God as well as Goddess Earth".

"The Vedas have a well defined structure. The first and the main part is the *samhitha*, the collection of *manthras*. The second part is Brahmanas, explanation or tutorials for the priests on how to use the *manthras*. The Brahmanas also include two other sections: Aranyaka and Upanishads. The former is meant for those who renounce the world with all its social responsibilities and retire to the forest. Aranyakas teach those who are in the stage of *vanaprastha* (forest life) methods of meditation based on symbolic interpretation of sacrificial rites. This enables them to perform *yagnas* and sacrificial rites at the mental level. The Upanishads are of more recent origin and represent the intellectual content of Vedas. They represent the evolution of the Hindu theology. Here we come across concepts like Brahman, the immanent God or the Supreme Eternal Soul, and Atman, the individual Soul. The Soul is the constant and indestructible factor all beings. While the body can age and die, the Soul lives on forever. It can take rebirth and thus continue the cycle of life and death. The practical aspect of this theology is that the body that hosts the Soul in the next birth depends on ones behaviour in the current life. Those who lead a righteous life following the path of righteousness [Dharma] will be born into a higher form of life. For ordinary people, the path is one of performing all the rituals prescribed in the Vedas. Relief from this endless cycle of birth and death is called *moksha*, the state in which the Atman becomes one with Brahman. This is considered the ultimate bliss".

"By studying the Vedas, we can learn about the society in which these works were composed. Here is a developing society with limited media of communication. Their interaction with the Divine consists of singing hymns of praise and worshiping anthropomorphic gods derived from forces of nature like fire, the sky and rain, and the rivers that could bring both prosperity and calamity to them. *Indra* was obviously the most important god, as he is mentioned 289 times in Rig Veda. He was considered the god of the skies, of thunder and rain, and god of war. He was particularly important as the god who released the rivers from the sky. Agni, *Indra's* twin brother comes second in popularity with 218 hymns addressed to him. He was thought as the representative of the Sun and was visible as the sacred fire used in rituals of purification. *Varuna*, the god of the waters and guardian of cosmic law of justice, is mentioned 146 times. Soma comes fourth with 123 mentions; this drink appears to be important in Vedic rituals. There is no mention in the Rig Veda of a hierarchy of gods. The obvious inference is that these gods evolved naturally as people learned to deal with natural forces like rain and thunder, sun and fire, and societal rules. As time passed, they identified more gods to be worshiped and more rituals to be performed. Celestial order with one or more principal deities and the the structure of a hierarchy with inter-relationships among various gods came later. More specifically, we do not find the triumvirate of Brahma, Vishnu and Shiva as well the incarnations of Vishnu in the four *Vedas*.

EPICS

"There are two epics composed in the Vedic period, which are part of the Hindu Scriptures. They are Ramayana and Mahabharata. The former is believed to have been composed by Valmiki many centuries ago and the latter by the sage Vyasa a few centuries later. Both works are orally transmitted down the generations, and modifications along the way cannot be ruled out. We will discuss the currently available versions".

"Ramayana is the story of Rama, the eldest son of King Dasaratha, who ruled over Kosala from its capital Ayodhya. The King had three wives - Kousalya, Kaikeyi and Soumitra. As the King was without children for a long time, he performed a fire sacrifice. As a consequence, the senior Queen, Koushalya gave birth to the first son, Ram. Kaikeyi, the second wife gave birth to the second son, Bharatha. Soumitra became mother of twin sons, Lakshmana and Shatrugna. The boys received good instructions in the Scriptures as well as in martial practices. Rama and Lakshmana received special training in the use of supernatural weaponry from Sage Vishwamithra, which they used to destroy demons that disturbed sacrificial rites. Prince Ram was an ideal son, and a firm believer in Dharma, the righteous way of life. He was also very popular as well as quite accomplished with bow and arrow. There was no doubt in anybody's mind that Ram would succeed Dasaratha when the latter vacated the throne. In a neighbouring kingdom of Mithila, King Jhanak organised the *Swayamvara* for his adopted daughter Sita. In Swayamvara function, all eligible princes from neighbouring kingdoms were invited as candidates to win the hand of the princess. The contest was the stringing of a heavy bow. Nobody could lift the bow, let alone string it. Rama, who was known as *ajanabahu (long-armed),* accomplished this feat with effortless ease. Sita now placed the garland she was carrying around Ram's neck, thus accepting him as her husband. Rama and his brothers formally married Jhanak's daughters in a big wedding function.

One day King Dasarata decided to retire to the forest to meditate, after handing over the reins of the State to his eldest son. This decision surprised nobody except Rama's step mother, Queen Kaikeyi, who wanted her son Bharata to be the king. She reminded the King of two boons he had granted to her some time earlier that she could ask anything and it would be given to her. Now her demand was that Ram should be banished to the forest for fourteen years and Bharatha installed as king in his place. Dasaratha had no choice but to hand over the Kingdom to Bharata to fulfill his promise. As an obedient son, Rama accepted his father's decision. When Rama prepared to go to the forest, Sita insisted on going with him, reminding him that it was her duty to look after her husband in the forest. Then Lakshmana also decided to join the party. When Bharata heard about the turn of events, he went to the forest to meet Rama. *Our custom is that the eldest son should succeed the father,* he said. *Please come back and rule over Kosala.* But Ram was clear that his first duty was to obey his father. He firmly told his brother to go back and rule over their Kingdom. So Bharatha took Ram's sandals, which he would place on the throne and rule on behalf of his brother, until the latter returned from his term in the forest.

Rama, Sita and Lahshmana settled down in their hermitage on the banks of Godavari, and started enjoying their forest life. At Panchavati forest, they got a visitor. She was Shoorpanakha, the sister of Ravana, the King of Lanka. When she failed to seduce the brothers, she attempted to kill Sita, Enraged, Lakshmana took his sword and cut off her nose and ears. Injured and humiliated, she approached her brother Khara, who mounted an attack on Rama's party with his demons. Rama annihilated them. Shoorpanakha then went back to Lanka and set about seeking revenge. She informed her brother Ravana that Rama and his beautiful wife were camping in the forest. Ravana took the help of a *rakshasa* (demon) with the name Maricha, who took the form of a golden deer to tempt Sita. She pleaded with Rama to capture the deer for her. Rama went after the deer after ensuring that his brother would protect Sita. As Rama did not return for some time, Lakshmana went to investigate; but before going, he drew a magic circle around Sita to make her safe so long as she remained within that. Ravana now took the form of an itinerant holy man, and begged for alms. The holy man tricked Sita into coming out of the magic circle to give him alms. In no time, Ravana got hold of Sita and took her to Lanka, where she lived in a garden and not in the royal palace. Neither his threats, nor his sweet talk had any effect on Sita's determination to keep away from him. She successfully resisted all attempts at seduction".

"Meanwhile, Rama along with Lakshmana went in search of Sita. He got the information from a vulture named Jadayu that she was abducted by Ravana. They traveled south and reached Kishkindha, the capital of a monkey kingdom, ruled by Vali. They met Sugriva, the brother of Vali, who thought he should have been the king. With the help of Hanuman, a leader of the monkeys, Rama killed Vali in a battle and restored the kingdom to Sugriva. After some dilly dallying, Sugriva sent search parties in all the four directions. The southern search party, led by Hanuman, learned that Sita was taken by Ravana to Lanka. Hanuman, using his supernatural powers, leaped across the sea to locate Sita. He found her sitting under an Ashoka tree. He showed her Rama's signet ring for identification and offered to take her back to Rama, but she refused as she did not want to be touched by any man other than her husband. However, Hanuman's presence was noted by the guards. Ravana devised a punishment for Hanuman, which consisted of winding cotton bands, dipped in oil around his tail and setting fire to it. As they wrapped the tail, it grew bigger and bigger. When it was lit at the end, the tail became shorter and shorter, remaining ahead of the fire. With the lit tail, Hanuman jumped from housetop to housetop, thus setting the capital on fire. Then he jettisoned the burning cloth by shrinking the tail to its original size and flew back to Rama and reported that Sita was well and waiting for him. Rama decided to go to Lanka to release his wife, with the help of Hanuman and his army. The problem was how to cross the sea. Hanuman and his colleagues solved this problem by building a bridge from the Indian continent to the island of Lanka over which the brothers marched their army into Lanka. Meanwhile, Vibhishana, the estranged brother of Ravana, joined the party. A fierce battle was joined which raged for days. In the end Rama killed Ravana and installed Vibhishana as the king in his place. Rama ordered that Sita be brought to him in the open court. In the presence of all the people, Rama asked Sita to undergo *agnipariksha* (trial by fire) in view of what some common people were saying about her purity. Sita unhesitatingly walked into the fire and walked out unscathed. Sita then accompanied Rama and Laksmana back to their hermitage in the forest. On completion of the exile period, they returned to Ayodhya where Rama was crowned as King. This was the beginning of Rama *Rajya* (Rama's Reign), a Kingdom ruled according to the principles of Dharma [righteousness]. Even after many years of this benign rule, questions about Sita's purity was raised by some common people. King Rama yielded to public pressure and banished Sita to the forest. Here sage Valmiki gave her refuge in his hermitage, where she gave birth to twin sons, Lava and Kusha. Valmiki took the responsibility of their training in various skills including martial arts. Then Rama performed *Aswamedha Yaga* (horse sacrifice), in which his horse was allowed to roam about the whole country. Anyone who blocked the horse was required to battle it out with the accompanying King. Those who permitted free passage became vassals who were required to pay tribute to the King. Rama, in his journey, ran into his twin sons who, having learned of their martial skills from Sage Valmiki, could match the skills of their father. Sita now appeared before Rama, and prayed to Mother Earth (*Prithvi*, her mother) who opened up and took her in to her bosom. Rama returned to Ayodhya with his twin sons and continued to rule until his death. Rama is taken as the role model for everyone to follow. He was an ideal son to his father, an ideal brother to his siblings, an ideal husband to his wife and ideal king who ruled by the principles of Dharma. Rama *Rajya* is the benchmark by which all Governments have to be measured."

MAHABAHRARTA

Shakuntala now took up the next epic for study. "Mahabharatha is the second epic of the Hindu Scriptures and the longer of the two. It is the story of the dynastic struggle between two sets of cousins for the throne of Hasthinapura, a kingdom which was located in the general geographic region of our university. It starts with King Shantanu who ruled over Hastinapura. He had a short-lived marriage with goddess Ganga, which produced a son by the name Devavratha who was later known as Bhishma, a great expert in martial arts. Later King Shantanu went on a hunting expedition and was infatuated by Satyavathy, daughter of the chief of fishermen, and asked her father for her hand in marriage. The father put a condition to this alliance: that any future son born in this wedlock would inherit the throne of Hasthinapura. Devavratha offered to renounce his claim to the throne to facilitate his father's marriage. To allay any lingering doubts about his progeny staking their claim to the kingdom, he took an additional vow of celibacy. Satyavathy presented two sons to Shantanu, who were named Chitrangada and Vichitravira. On Santanu's death, Chitrangada succeeded him, but did not live very long. His brother took over the reins of. Hastinapura. But the young ruler was not invited to the Swayamvara of the three daughters of the King of Kashi - Amba, Ambika and Ambalika. His uncle Bhishma went there in order to abduct the three princesses. To achieve his goal, he had to defeat the King of Shalva. Ambika and Ambalika agreed to marry King Vichitravira. But Amba wanted to marry the King of Shalva, who rejected her because of his defeat by Bhishma. Amba returned to Bhishma to marry him, but he could not do it because of his vow of celibacy. She vowed to avenge her humiliation and later took birth as Shikhandi who caused the death of Bhishma. When King Vichitravira died young without any issue, his mother asked Vyasa to have intercourse with the widows and produce successors to the King. Ambika closed her eyes on seeing Vyasa and her son, Dhritarashtra, was born blind. When Ambalika's turn came, she turned pale, and her son Pandu was born jaundiced and unhealthy. Vyasa agreed to try again, but this time the queens sent their maid as substitute, and a healthy son named Vidura was born. He grew up to be a wise statesman.

Vidura blocked the coronation of the older prince, when he came of age, arguing that a blind man could not be king, as he was unable see his subjects. Thus Pandu became the king. Pandu took two wives, Kunti and Madri, while Dhritarashtra married Gandhari, a princess from Gandhara. Gandhari blindfolded herself permanently so that she could feel what her husband was going through. She gave birth to hundred children who became known as Kauravas. King Pandu went hunting in the forest and an arrow from his bow hit sage Kindama, who cursed him that if he engaged in sexual pleasure he would die. His wife Kunti, however, found a way out. She had a boon from sage Durvasa that she could invoke any god by using a special Manthra and get pregnant. She used the Manthra to have sons by Dharma, the god of justice, Vayu the wind god and Indra the lord of the skies. Kunti shared her Manthra with the junior queen who gave birth to the twins, Nakula and Sahadeva, through the Ashwini twins. Madri enjoyed the carnal pleasure with her husband and this caused Pandu's death on account of the curse of Kindama. Overcome by remorse for causing Pandu's death, Madri jumped on the funeral pyre of her husband and ended her life. Kunti became the only parent for the five brothers known as 'the Pandavas'. Mahabharatha is the story of the rivalry between the Kauravas and the Pandavas, which led to the Kurukshetra war.

Kunti returned to Hastinapura with the Pandavas, after Pandu's death. Though the Kauravas were hundred in number, Yudhishtira was born earlier than Duryodhana, the senior most of the Kauravas. On the seniority consideration, Dhritarashtra made Yudhishtira the crown prince, but this was not liked by the Kauravas. They hatched a plan, along with their cunning uncle Shakuni, to eliminate the Pandavas. They built a palace of wax for their rivals to stay. Alerted by their uncle Vidura, the Pandavas managed to dig a tunnel out of this palace, and escaped before it was burnt. But the Kauravas thought they had seen the last of their rivals. While the Pandavas were thus in hiding, they heard of a Swayamvara arranged for Draupadi, the princess of Panchala. The competition was to to string a heavy bow and hit a moving target in the form of the eye of a fish, viewing it through its reflection in the water below. The Pandavas decided to enter the competition. Arjuna was the only competitor who could string the bow and hit the target. Thus he won the competition as well as Draupadi's hand in marriage. For this, he had to reveal his identity. The Pandavas reported to their mother that Arjuna won a trophy at the competition in Panchala and asked her see it. Without bothering to see the trophy, Kunti asked her children to share the prize equally, whatever it was. Thus Draupadi became the wife all the five Pandavas.

Now that the Pandavas came out in the open, they were welcomed back to Hastinapura. Dhritarashtra and his advisors tried to broker peace by splitting the Kingdom into two and giving the new territories in the east to the Pandavas. King Yudhishtira built a beautiful new capital city there and named it Indraprastha. The new kingdom became quite prosperous, particularly in comparison to Hastinapura. Yudhishtira then performed an *Aswmedha Yaga*, or Horse Sacrifice, which made him the King of Kings with supremacy over all other Kings. He then invited all the kings for a celebration. Kauravas were also extended an invitation to the party. Duryodhana was green with envy. Seeing the polished and reflecting floor, Duryodhana thought it was a pond filled with water, and hesitated to walk on it. Later, when he was shown a pool filled to the brim with water, he tried walking on it and got thoroughly drenched. Watching this scene, Draupadi had a hearty laughter. Duryodhana nursed a special grudge against her on this count. Back in Hastinapura, the wily Shakuni proposed that Yudhishtira should be challenged to play a game of dice which he was confident that Kauravas would win. Duryodhana erected a special hall for the contest and invited all the kings of nearby kingdoms to the great event. Yudhishtira lost all the rounds of throwing of the dice, as Shakuni had made sure that the dice was loaded. One by one he pledged and lost all his wealth as well as his kingdom. "Don't you want to continue?" asked Duryodhana. "I have nothing more to pledge", replied Yudhishtira. "You have your brothers", countered his tormentor. "Well, I will play", said the gambler. Thus he lost his brothers, one by one, who were stripped of their weapons and made to kneel beside servants. Now all that was left was he himself, and finally his wife, and lost them all. The Kauravas decided to enforces their rights including the ownership of Draupadi. She refused to accompany the messengers of Duryodhana. So he sent his brother Dussasana to fetch her. He dragged her by her hair and brought her to the hall. They started disrobing her in front of the whole court, but her honour was saved by an unseen Krishna, who miraculously provided enough length of cloth to cover her, however much cloth Dussasana pulled it out. Finally he fell down exhausted without reaching his goal. Draupadi now appealed to the King, addressing him as her father-in-law. "Why are you keeping quiet, when I am dishonoured in public? Won't you help your daughter-in-law, in her distress? When Yudhishtira lost himself in the dice game, he had no right to offer me as stake. What is done to me is unlawful". At last, Dhritarashtra spoke: "You are free, Draupadi. Further, you can ask me any boon". Duryodhana protested, but was overruled. Draupadi demanded Yudhishtira's freedom as her boon. After granting this, the King offered her a second boon. She demanded the freedom of Bhima, Arjuna, Nakula and Sshadeva and this was also granred. The King offered her one more boon, but she refused, saying: "When my husbands are free, I don't need any boon. They will get me whatever I want". But the King ordered the restoration of everything that Pandavas lost, and asked them to go peacefully back to Indraprastha".

One of the students raised his hand to signal a question. Shakuntala permitted him to go ahead and ask his question. "Madam, you haven't told us who Krishna is", said the young student. "Thank you for reminding me", she said, and continued. "Krishna is the divine factor in our narration. As we proceed further, you will see that he reveals himself as God incarnate. Krishna was born as the son of Yadava chief Vasudeva and his wife Devaki. Years before Krishna was born, Devaki's brother Kamsa usurped the Kingdom of Surasena after imprisoning his father, Ugrasena, who was the ruling king. Believing an astrologer's prediction that his end would come by the hands of Devaki's son, Kamsa killed the first six sons delivered by Devaki. When Krishna was born, Vasudeva sent the baby secretly to Gokula to be brought up by Yashoda and Nanda. Nanda was a cow herdsman and thus young Krishna grew up with cows, milk, butter and *Gopikas* (milkmaids), and had lots of fun fooling around with them and stealing butter. During this period he killed demoness Puthana who was sent by Kamsa in the form of a wet nurse with instructions to finish off Krishna. He also killed Kalia, the serpent king, who poisoned the bathing *ghat* where gopikas bathed. Mahabharata describes in detail the frolics and mischief's of young Krishna and this has endeared this *Balamuralihrishna* (young Krishna with the flute) to his devotees. In fact, the youthful Krishna with a flute in hand is the ubiquitous image of this deity. When Krishna grew up to be a young man, he went back to Surasena, killed Kamsa and reinstated the old king Ugrasena on the throne. This Kingdom gradually became weak from attacks by Jarasandha, King of the Magadha Kingdom. So Krishna persuaded Yadavas to move south and later established a new Kingdom at Dwaraka. He became friends with Arjuna and his brothers, who were his cousins, as the sons of his aunt Kunthi. When Subhadra, a Yadava princess eloped with Arjuna, Krishna persuaded the angry Yadavas not to pursue the couple. 'There is no disgrace in conciliation', he said. He used the same tactful approach to keep the discordant Yadavas of Dwaraka together to establish and maintain the Dwaraka Kingdom".

"Krishna married eight princesses, who became known as his queens. The most important among them was Rukmini, whom he abducted from Vidarbha. She had overheard the plans of her brother Rukmi, the crown prince of Vidarbha, to marry her off to Shishupala, a supporter of King Jarasandra, and sent an urgent message to Krishna to come and save her. Krishna went from Dwaraka in his chariot, and picked up Rukmini at a prearranged spot. In order to escape with Rukmini he had to fight both Shishupala and Rukmi. The second most favourite queen was Satyabhama. Jambavati, Nagnajiti, Kalindi. Mitravina, Bhadra and Lakshmana were the other queens. In addition, he acquired 16100 wives when he saved them from Demon *Narakasura*. The story is that these women were held captive by the demon. On hearing of their plight, Krishna went and defeated Narakasura and freed all of them. However the freed women complained to Krishna that they had nowhere to go, as their families would not take them back, nor would anybody marry them, because of the bad name of being in Narakasura's palace. So Krishna married all of them and brought them back to Dwaraka. There he built a palace for each one of them and appointed servants to take care of them. The questioner raised his hand again, and asked: 'How could Krishna be a good husband to 16100 wives and eight queens?" Shakuntala replied: "The answer to that depends on whom you ask the question. The answer given by devotees, who are experts in Hindu Scriptures, is that Krishna as God could split himself into 16100 Krishnas and play his role as husband to each one of the 16100 wives. The underlying principle is that God can do anything. You are free to question that." The questioner was on his feet again. He said: "I question the authenticity of the scripture as well as God's willingness to perform this feat for the purpose enjoying the intimate company of so many women".

"Let us go back to our story", Shakuntala continued. "Duryodhana protested vigorously against the award given by Dhritarashtra, and even threatened to go on fast. Filial loyalty won, and Pandavas were asked to return for a second dice game. Here the stake was that the losing party would go into exile for twelve years, followed by one year during which they should live incognito. If they were discovered during this period, they would be required to go into exile for another twelve years. Yudhishtira lost all the rounds this time also, as Shakuni was still throwing the dice. Thus Pandavas went into exile for twelve years. It gave them the taste of a different kind of life. They travelled all across northern India, visiting places of pilgrimage and interacting with sages as well as common people. There was no hardship, as they traveled with their entourage. They also met kings and forged alliances which came in handy in the future course of events. Draupadi did make it a bit difficult for her husbands, especially Yudhishtira, for the ignominy that she had to suffer, but that was more like a minor aside. The Pandavas spent their thirteenth year in disguise in the court of Virata, who was a minor king. Yudhishtira became the king's tutor in dice games. Bhima was the chief cook in charge of the royal kitchen. Draupadi signed up as the queen's hair dresser. Arjuna, in the form of a transvestite, became the dance teacher of the princess. The year passed uneventfully, but they were discovered just after they completed the year.

The Pandavas returned to claim their kingdom, but Duryodhana was in no mood to oblige. He claimed that Pandavas were detected before the year was over. War between the cousins became inevitable. Negotiations were indeed held, with the seniors getting into this act. Krishna suggested a compromise, but Duryodhana would not budge an inch. Krishna came on a peace mission with the proposal to give Indraprastha or at least five villages to the Pandavas, but Duryodhana refused saying that no land of even the size of a pin would be given to the Pandava cousins. Krishna then told Yudhishtira that war was the only way out to uphold the principles of virtue and righteousness, and went back to Dwaraka. So both sides prepared for war, and cobbled up alliances. Both of them approached Krishna for his support. Duryodhana went first and finding Krishna sleeping sat near the head of the bed. Arjuna reached later, but humbly sat at the foot of the bed. When Krishna woke up, he saw Arjuna first and hence was given the first choice. Krishna said that he was equally related to both parties, and hence he would put his large and well trained Narayani Sena (army) on one side and he himself, unarmed, on the other side, and let them choose. Arjuna chose Lord Krishna whom he asked to be his charioteer. Duryodhana was happy to take the Narayani Sena. So Krishna became Arjuna's charioteer. Balarama, Krishna's elder brother, was so disgusted with the turn of events that he left the scene."

"Both sides found allies to support them in the war. There were 18 armies on the side of the Kauravas, while the Pandavas had 12 armies. They faced each other in Kurukshetra, the field of Kurus. Before the war began, Arjuna asked his charioteer to take him to the middle of the field, between the two armies. Arjuna looked ahead and saw the vast armies. He was able to identify many faces. He told Krishna: *I see my Pithamaha (grandfather), my cousins and my friends facing us, Krishna. It cannot be lawful to kill them. I do not want any part in this war.* Krishna replied: 'If your attitude is dispassionate, and you are acting lawfully regardless of consequences, there can be no blame on you'. But Arjuna was not satisfied. *All these people are going to die, Krishna,* countered Arjuna. *I do not want to be responsible for their death.* Krishna now explained to his friend:"We are all instruments of Dharma. All of us have to face the consequences of our Karma, which is the accumulated effect of all our past and present births. We have all been hurtling to this battle for numerous births, deaths and rebirths. The difference between you and me is that I remember all those births, but you don't". Arjuna looked at Krishna and asked: "Who are you really, Krishna?" Suddenly there was a flash of light, brighter than a thousand suns, and Arjuna was staring at Krishna's *Vishvaroopam*, his Cosmic Form. There in one glimpse he saw the entire universe with all the stars and planets, all gods and demons, all the sages and saints, all that was past and present and what was yet to happen including the gory details what would happen in the ensuing battle. There was Krishna, standing tall as the mountain, black as night, his eyes blazing, as he waded through rivers of blood and mangled corpses including that of Duryodhana. Arjuna asked Krishna to stop and just become his friend. Krishna obliged and then continued to advice Arjuna. "You have to understand, Arjuna, that you are not responsible for the deaths of these people, as they are already dead. Their actions in their past births have predetermined their fate. You and I are born on earth to exterminate the wicked and establish a righteous order. In every birth and life each of us have to do our duty and those who do it selflessly out of their love for me, and not for any private gain, they will break the cycle of birth and death, and come to rest in my (*Narayana's*) perfection. Now you Arjuna must fight as a warrior, because of your steadfast love for me." Krishna's advice to Arjuna in the battle field on doing his selfless duty (*nishkamakarma*) with its accompanying theology is called Bhagawath Githa and constitutes an important part of Mahabharata. It is in fact Hindu Theology. Krishna summarised his mission in the following verse, followed by my free translation:

Paritranaya Sadhunam
Vinasaya ca Dushkritam
Dharma samsthapanarthaye
Sambhavami Yuge Yuge
To protect the righteous
To exterminate the wicked
To establish the righteous system
I take birth eon after eon.

This directly leads us to the Hindu concept of *avatar* or reincarnations of Narayana, also known as Vishnu. Elsewhere Krishna acknowledges the fact that in an earlier birth he was Rama. The consolidation of the concept of God in this manner is rather recent, but it brings in the much needed order in the Hindu pantheon of gods. Brahma is the creator, Vishnu is the sustainer, and Shankar (also known as Shiva) is the destroyer. Vishnu takes birth periodically (once in an eon) to re-establish order based on Dharma. There are efforts underway to identify other *avatars*".

"The war began amidst a cacophony of conch shells and war cry of the troops. Before it began, both sides agreed on a *Dharma Yudha* - Just War. The rules prohibited fighting at night, proportionate armaments (chariot for a chariot, cavalry against cavalry, armed men not to fight unarmed ones, women and children to be excluded etc.). But as war progressed, both sides violated the rules. When the war was joined, Arjuna noted that Bhishma Pithamaha was the commander-in-chief of the Kaurava Army. He was not only an outstanding warrior skilled in the operation of many weapons, but also a consummate strategist. Moreover, he had with him a boon that he could choose the time of his death. He was fighting against the Pandavas not for his love for Kauravas but to fulfill a vow he had taken that he would be loyal to the Kuru throne which was now occupied by Dhritharshtra. He went into the battle with all earnestness, killing thousands of soldiers and scores of commanders of the opposite side. But he remained invincible. The carnage went on for nine days making a big dent on the Pandava Army. Naturally Krishna was approached for a solution. He told Arjuna that Bhishma would not only not fight a woman, but would lay down his arms when a woman approached. Bhishma confirmed that this applied even if the person was a woman in the previous birth. So Arjuna took Shikhandi in his chariot. Seeing Shikhandi approaching, Bhishma got out of his chariot and put down his arms. This enabled Arjuna to fire multiple arrows on Bhishma's back, which made a bed of arrows as the latter fell back. Bhishma, who could choose his time of death, decided to delay his death until the autumn solstice as that would be a more auspicious time to go straight to heaven. When Yudhishtira visited him, he gave him a lecture on the qualities expected of a King".

"At the fall of Bhishma, Drona took over the command of the Army. Dronacharya was the teacher who taught martial arts to both Pandavas and Kauravas. He himself was an astute warrior and an able strategist. Since it was essential to eliminate him to win the war, the Pandavas decided to exploit Drona's only weakness: his great love for his son, Ashwatama. When Drona was mortally wounded, he refused to die and asked for his son. So Pandavas enacted a drama to fool the old warrior. Bhima killed an elephant named Ashwatama and shouted at the top of his voice: 'Ashwatama is dead'. But Drona insisted on hearing the news from Yudhishtira, who would speak only the truth. So Yudhishtira said quite loudly: "Ashwatama is dead", and then continued in a low voice: "the elephant"(rather, *naro va kunjaro va,* meaning that it could be man or animal*).* Believing Yudhishtira, Drona succumbed to death. Thereupon Karna took over the command, but could not stand up to Arjuna, because he carried the curse of forgetting his skills when they were most needed. Karna fought valiantly on the first day and inflicted heavy losses on the Pandava Army. The next day he defeated the Pandava brothers Sahadeva and Nakula in battle, but spared their lives. He found his match in Arjuna, but had to request for a pause when his chariot wheel got stuck in mud. Krishna asked Arjuna not to yield, reminding him of Karna's ruthlessness to Abhimanyu (Arjuna's son) under similar conditions. Arjuna shot his arrow and decapitated Karna. Ashwatama now came to the forefront, with the motivation of avenging his father's death. He vowed to kill all Pandavas. Disregarding all rules, he attacked the Pandava camp at night killing five upapandavas (five children of Draupadi), mistaking them for Pandavas. Ashwatama also killed most of the people in the Pandava camp. On the eighteenth day, Yudhishtira killed King Shalya, the new commander. Meanwhile, Bhima challenged Duryodhana for a duel using their favourite weapon, the Mace (*Gadda*). They fought hard for a long time on the eighteenth day under supervision of Balarama who had by now returned to the scene. With neither contestant winning. Krishna pointed to his thigh hinting to Bhima where he should attack. Krishna knew that this was the weak spot. Bhima hit a mighty blow on the enemy's thigh, breaking the thigh bone. This way he not only killed the enemy, but also fulfilled his promise to Draupadi to break Duryodhana's thigh bone for humiliating her. Bhima killed all the remaining Kaurava brothers. Seeing the carnage, Gandhari cursed Krishna for not stopping the war which he knew would end like this, with all her sons dead. The curse was that Krishna would see a similar end to his Yadava family. Krishna accepted the curse, knowing that the Yadavas would have a similar fate on account of their internal strife. In the battlefield, Ashwatama attacked Arjuna and rained arrow for arrow. Finally as a last resort, he fired the *Brahmasthra* (Divine Arrow), the use of which Dronacharya taught only to these two pupils. Arjuna also shot his Divine *Asthra*. It was feared that if these two met, it would mean the end of the earth. So Veda Vyasa himself appeared in the sky and ordered the two combatants two withdraw the Divine Brahmasthra. Arjuna complied immediately, but Ashwathama could not, as withdrawal of the fired missile was not taught to him. He aimed it at the unborn baby in the womb of Uttara, the wife of Abhimanyu. He obviously meant to kill the unborn child, so that Pandavas would have no heir left. However, Krishna revived the baby, and cursed Ashwathama that he would wander in the wilderness without friends or even human contact. The baby would grow up to be Parikshit, the successor of Yudhishtira as the next king of the Kuru dynasty. Meanwhile, Krishna declared the war over, as no Kaurava was left".

"At the end of the war, there were only twelve survivors - the five Pandavas, Krishna, Stayaki, Yuyutsu, Kripa, Kritavarma, Ashwathama and Vrishakethu, the son of Karna. Yudhishtira was crowned king of Hastinapura. This was followed by a yagna, which established him as the premier king of the whole region. After ruling for thirty six years, the Pandavas lost interest in royal palace and power, and anointed Parikshit as the King. Renouncing everything, they wore rags and skins, and journeyed to Himalayas to climb their way to heaven. One by one, Draupadi and the brothers fell as they climbed. As each one fell, Yudhishtira explained the reason for their fall. He said that Draupadi was partial to Arjuna, Nakula and Sahaveva were proud of their looks, and

Bhima and Arjuna were proud of their skills. Finally Yudhishtira was left with a stray dog that accompanied them. The dog turned out to be Yama Dharmaraj, who took him to the underworld to see his brothers and wife. Yamaraj explained to him that any king should visit the underworld once and assured him that his brothers and wife would soon join him in heaven. Yamaraj then guided Yudhishtira to heaven".

Shakuntala now concluded her presentation: "Thus we see the evolution of Hindu thought regarding God, starting with Rig Veda, Sama Veda, Yajur Veda, to the epics Ramayana and Mahabharta. From the epics we recognise that their heroes Rama and Krishna are gods. In fact, we learn from Lord Krishna that Lord Vishnu takes birth as avatars or incarnations, eon after eon to protect the righteous, to annihilate the wicked, and to establish the system of Dharma. Lord Rama, the hero of Ramayana was also an *avatar*. Balarama, the elder brother of Krishna is also said to be an *avatar*. The list *is* incomplete as yet."

Shakuntala explained to her audience that she presented the Vedas and the epic stories as she understood them. "It is widely believed that the Scriptures were composed by Sages of great wisdom, and orally passed on unchanged from generation to generation. But it is possible that the texts could have been modified along the way, particularly as language evolved. Language, after all, is the medium of communication. As language develops and gets richer, communication becomes better. There are indications that this has actually happened, making the hymns and the legends more coherent. Thus the epics are unlikely to be the works of single authors like Valmiki and Vyasa, but the result of progressive evolution."

Shakuntala was quite open to questions during her presentation. However, the open discussion at the end was most vigorous and exciting. At the beginning of the discussion session, Shakuntala declared that the entire course was open for discussion, not just her presentation on Hinduism. There were a number of questions on authenticity of the Scriptural Texts. Shakuntala pointed out that it was difficult to check the authenticity of oral traditions which are not written down. This is because only the current version is available. The fact that they were in the form of verses, set to well defined metre and rhythm, did not preclude modifications over centuries. To a question on the divine origin of the scripture, her reply was that whatever one could glean out of the available material suggested an evolution in human concept of God. "Rig

Veda, which was the oldest of the texts, invoked gods representing the forces of nature like fire, sun, thunder and lightning, winds and rain etc. But later we find a consolidation of these gods into a structure, with a triumvirate of Brahma, Vishnu and Shiva at the centre and all the smaller deities subservient to them. All the Divine Beings which took human or animal form are *Avatars* or incarnations of Vishnu".

A young man named Kannan got up and vehemently protested against the description of the people of the Southern Kingdom as monkeys in Ramayana. The story, he said, was obviously written by people who had never even visited the South. "My father", he continued, "comes from the South and lives and works in the great port city of Muchiripattinam, called Muziris by the Greek. There is no city anywhere in Bharat, or for that matter anywhere in world, that can compare with Muchiripattinam". 'How did you get here?' asked several voices. "Well, my father is a Cheran, who works with the Chera King in the spice trade which brings ships from many parts of the world. My mother is from the north and she married my father when she came to Muchiripattinam for a visit with her parents and brother. When I grew up, my mother sent me to her brother (my uncle) for study at this university. Of course, I am glad I came, but will return to Muchiripattinam when I graduate". Shakuntala suggested that Ramayana should be taken as a story, which describes an ideal king like Rama. "How do you consider him ideal", countered Kannan. "Look at the way he treated his wife. Just because some people gossiped, he humiliated her and subjected her to trial by fire (*agnipariksha*) twice. A king who treats his wife so badly cannot be just to his subjects".

Another student asked why a hero like Yudhishtira could repeat his mistake of not checking whether the dice was loaded. The first game itself should have made him suspect foul play, for one cannot lose every throw of dice. Or should we conclude that the man of Dharma was also foolish. Why didn't his brothers protest against being pawned in the game? After all, Yudhishtira did not own them. What could Yudhishtira have taught King Virata about dice game in which he failed so miserably? Shakuntala's answer was that she was only reporting what Mahabharata has said. It is up to each listener to interpret it in his own way.

Another set of questions related to the nature of God as revealed himself through the Scriptures. Why did the incarnations of god like Rama and Krishna want to marry and have children? Why was Krishna so keen on romancing girls like gopikas? Aren't these just human needs or weaknesses? If Rama was god, then he must have known about Ravana's plan to abduct Sita and could have foiled it. If Krishna took birth to exterminate wicked people like Kauravas, then he could have achieved it without causing so much bloodshed. Even in the worst case, the carnage could have been limited to the really wicked men, and tens of thousands of innocent lives could have been saved. Krishna even justified crooked methods like the use of Shikhandi to mortally wound Bhishma and making Yudhishtira to tell a lie to cause the death of Drona. Some critics even went to the extent of saying that the epics were well composed dramas meant to entertain the masses and questioned their value as Scripture. Shakuntala pointed out that her Course was only an academic study of the scriptural texts, and not an exercise in promoting a religion. Her position as an academician was that all scriptures depict human effort to understand God, and not God's revelation of ultimate truth.

At this point, Shakuntala requested Yeshua to sum up the entire course. Yeshua got up and said that Shakuntala had already summed up the Course when she explained her academic position. As faculty members leading a course on religions, neither Shakuntala nor he was interested in promoting one religion or other. During the course of their preparations, they had come to the conclusion that there was only one God. "Then why are the gods of different religions so different? It is difficult to believe that the same God donned different forms in revealing himself to different people. The only possible conclusion is that different cultures, as they developed, made different models of God, consistent with the stage of development of their languages. These models were depicted through hymns of prayer and praise, as well as through drama meant for entertainment and information. The more articulate among them set their text to verse, making them easier to remember and recite. But none of the gods is perfect, as imperfections arising from human limitations are clearly seen in each. The reason why gods are worshiped, adored and showered with offerings is clearly their superhuman abilities to heal, to bless the devotees by fulfilling their desires and giving assistance in defeating enemies. But for this, it is doubtful if any god would have had a large following. This may also be the reason why Brahma has hardly any temple dedicated to him, whereas Vishnu and his avatars have myriads of temples in their names. Even their lieutenants like Hanuman have temples dedicated to them. The priests or *pujaries* who mediate on behalf of the supplicant also benefit. The priests everywhere managed to negotiate an important place in society in proportion to the public perception of their influence with god."

"Every religion has its scriptures and epics. For example, the Hindus have Ramayana and Mahabharata, the Greeks have Odyssey and Ulysses, and Jews have Tanaka. These epics have an important role in communication. It must be recognised that the most effective communication is through images. For Hindus the word Rama invokes the image of an ideal king, Sita stands for an ideal wife, and Hanuman for an ideal follower of the master. Yudhishtira was known for honesty and justice, and Narada for cunning etc. In Jewish Tanaka, Adam is the father of human race, Noah as the survivor of the great flood, Abraham the patriarch who followed the ideal of one God, Moses the law giver, and David and Solomon great kings. When one mentions these commonly known names, the whole imagery of their depiction comes to the mind of the listener and hence communication becomes possible in much fewer words. Thus, if you want to communicate with masses in Hindu areas, you must use imagery from Hindu scriptures, whereas if you want to communicate with Jewish masses, you must use imagery from the Tanaka. In fact, this is what I propose to do when I go back to my homeland and address Jewish masses".

"Our academic statements should not be taken to mean that we are against God or religion. What is the real nature of God, and how he holds the universe and all that is in it together, is something very difficult to comprehend. It is unlikely that he looks like a human being and that he has emotions like anger, vengeance, ego, love, hate etc. Perhaps Bhagwath Gita's advice to eschew *Kama* (lust), *Krodha* (rage), *Lobha* (greed) and *Mada* (arrogance) suggests that God does not have these human weaknesses. However, any model that we make of god would be necessarily based on human characteristics, because that is what we are familiar with. Different models have sprung up in different cultures, like Yahweh, Vishnu, Shiva, etc. If we understand that these models are only a means for focusing on God, and not an absolute description, then we can live in harmony with other religious groups. If on the other hand, we insist that ours is the right model, and others are wrong, we end up living perennially in strife. This is the message that we want to leave with you at the end of the course."

There was silence in the audience, which was followed by thunderous applause. A young man got up and said: "Sir, we are greatly enlightened by this Course and we marvel at your wisdom and your universal message. I have one last question: "In Buddhism, we are taught not to question the enlightened vision of the Shakyamuni, but to follow the path that he has laid out. Will you kindly tell us how to reconcile this with your teaching?" There was a gasp in the audience. Many wondered how this young teacher would handle this tricky question, which amounts to taking on Bhagwan Buddha. Even Shakuntala had a worried look, as she wanted her friend to handle this well. Yeshua was the picture of composure. He turned to the questioner and said:"If you are following the path prescribed by Buddha, please continue to do that. It can only do you good. But please do not despise others who may follow a different path". But the young man persisted. "Sir, most of us here greatly admire your message of harmony. In order to practice that, it is necessary for us to know whether there is any imperfection in Shakyamuni's logic". Shakuntala was visibly uncomfortable with the turn that the discussion was taking. Yeshua should know that they were in the heartland of Buddhism. Obviously, he could not speak against Bhagwan Buddha's teachings. Then how would he extricate himself? As Yeshua started speaking everybody listened in rapt attention. "Buddha Shakyamuni is doubtless the most recent of a few great thinkers that this country has produced. His teachings are based on the fundamental precept that all living beings are caught in an endless cycle of birth and death. Depending upon the good or bad deeds in the present life and the countless births before the present one, each one of us will take a higher or lower form of life in the next birth. All of you here have learned this from childhood and hence accept it without question. But I come from a different culture and religion and, therefore, I can look at this assumption dispassionately. If I were to be born as a fly in the next birth, how can that fly retain in its tiny brain all my consciousness and the account of my karma? We now know that it is the brain that carries the memory and that the higher forms of life are equipped with bigger brains and therefore bigger memories. Further, there is no proof that the fly faces the same moral dilemmas that we face. All that I am saying is that other cultures or civilisations may not accept the basic assumptions without proof. That should not be taken against them. Therefore, my advice is that you follow your chosen path, but remember that other paths are also possible. So long as you are a homogeneous culture these issues may not be noticeable. But if and when you have, among you, a sizeable minority belonging to a different culture or religion, problems surface. How you treat your minority groups or honest dissenters will determine your statesmanship and strife-free governance. The best way in my opinion is to separate State and

Religion. All people, regardless of their religion, should get the same treatment from the King". Kannan was already on his feet. He said: "Sir, I thank you for bringing up this subject. In Muchiripattinam, one can see the value addition that a small minority community has brought to our society. We have a small community of Jews who have come with the spice trade. They have been put in charge of weighing and packing spices. This was criticised by some people, but the King was firm on this arrangement as he felt that these people were honest and could converse with the traders coming from overseas in their language. My mother loves to visit the quaint little shops of these Jews and finds value in their merchandise. You have now given me a philosophical basis for nurturing this diversity". Yeshua said: "I hope that sometime in the future I will have the opportunity to visit your city and find out for myself the harmony there. On Kannan's practical note of harmony between cultures in the southern tip of this continent, I declare this course as over". There were a few moments of silence when Yeshua finished, which seemed like infinity to Shakuntala. Then the first questioner got up and said: "I salute you sir, for your wisdom. Your path is the only one which will bring harmony and peace". His last words were drowned in the applause.

CHAPTER 6

A Picnic to Margala Hills

After completing his assignment to conduct the course on comparative religion in association with Shakuntala, Yeshua sought an appointment with Guru Shantideva to ascertain whether he could leave for Palestine. The appointment was readily given. Yeshua pointed out that it was over ten years since he left his native Palestine to pursue higher studies in Taxila. He said: 'I learned much during my stay - from languages to Buddhism and healing. The course in comparative religion was a unique opportunity. I am truly grateful to the University, and more particularly to you, Guru Shantideva, for this wonderful chance to learn. However, the time has come for me to return to my people". Yeshua explained his mission to the Guru. He intended to go back and reinterpret to his fellow Jews their own religion. Their religion had become just a mechanical observance of the old laws. In this mission, what he learned in Taxila will play a major role. Yeshua acknowledged the fact that Guru Shantideva expected him to stay on for two years. However, he wanted to leave now for two reasons. It was only natural that his family wanted to see him after ten long years. He was also eager to see them. Moreover, he was getting messages from back home that things were coming to a boil and the opportune moment for him to start his mission had already arrived. Guru Shantideva patiently listened to Yeshua without interrupting him. Then he said that he considered himself fortunate to have had a brilliant and focused student like Yeshua. For records, he said, Yeshua was at the top of his class in all subjects. The course in comparative religion was the crowning glory of his achievements. It was impossible to find a replacement for him. The Acharya suggested that Yeshua should think it over for a week, and then communicate to him his final decision.

As Yeshua came out of the Guru's office, Shakuntala was waiting for him. They walked in silence for some time, and then sat down on one of the stone benches thoughtfully provided along the walkway. "The Guru was very nice to me; he had only positive things to say about me", said Yeshua in response to Shakuntala's questioning expression. "Tell me what he said about your mission", enquired Shakuntala. "He said that my mission was noble, but he had to consider the continuation of our course in the next academic year. He gave me one week's time to think it over and let him know my final decision", replied Yeshua. "Even I have to think about my partner to continue this course. As it is practically impossible to find one, the best solution is for you to marry me and stay on here for the rest of your life" said Shakuntala, snuggling close to him. "What are you doing, Shaku? Passersby will see us", chided Yeshua. "Let them see that I love you", she said defiantly. "Shakuntala, we are teachers. We are expected to set a good example", countered Yeshua. "Since when is sitting close to one's beloved a bad example?" asked the irate lady in love. Now she got up and pulled Yeshua up by hand, saying: "now you come home with me for a cup of tea; otherwise I will kiss you in public". Yeshua meekly followed her.

Her house was the standard university quarters that was allotted to her father as the head of the School of Languages. Unlike the older Schools, Language School was more contemporary in style and was built with stone blocks. Shakuntala made tea quickly and brought it in a tray of two cups along with some snacks. She put it on a stone table in front of Yeshua, and sat beside him. "Yeshua, I know that you love me. Why don't you marry me and settle down here?" "There is nothing better that I would like to do so happily. You are the most intelligent and the most beautiful woman I have ever met, and I love you deeply. The problem is that I have a mission, which is more important to me than anything else. It is an all consuming passion that has taken hold of me from my teen years. I cannot rest until I have tried it out", replied Yeshua without the show of any emotion. "Do as you wish, but remember one thing. I have installed your image in my heart. It will remain there whether you accept me or reject me"; her words came heavy with emotion, and she was obviously fighting hard to remain in control. "There is no question of rejecting you ever", replied Yeshua. "If I ever marry, you will be my bride. But please understand that I am going on a dangerous mission which may cost my life. But if I manage to survive, I promise you that I will come and get you". His voice was also quite emotional. Shakuntala snuggled close to him, and asked: "Why do you have to go on this dangerous mission? Stay back here, and we will have a good life together. I promise to make you happy", she said. "I know you will. But please understand that this mission has taken hold of me from a young age. I want to make my people understand that the principles behind their religion are more important than following the prescribed rules. It would be wonderful if I succeed. If I fail, let us hope that I can back to you alive. But I hate the thought of leaving you after marriage", said Yeshua. He then suggested that they leave the topic and enjoy each other's company.

"Tell me Shakuntala, how did you get such luxuriant black hair? It is so beautiful", asked Yeshua inserting his hand into the bushy hair. *This is the first time he has touched me*, thought Shakuntala. *Let this magic moment last forever.* But she answered his question easily, because she had been asked this before. "I owe my hair to my mother and my grandmother. My maternal grandfather was from a royal family. He was neither the king nor the heir apparent, which position rightly belonged to his elder brother. My grandfather was sent on a mission to the South, ostensibly to scout for new territories which could be annexed. Only later he came to know that the whole thing was a ruse by his elder brother to keep him away when the latter usurped power. When my grandfather came back, he found that his father, the King, had died under mysterious circumstances and his elder brother had become the King. During his sojourn in the South, my grandfather and his army detachment camped near an *Ashram* (hermitage). The head of the ashram had a beautiful daughter, with whom my grandfather fell in love. It is said that it was her thick black hair that attracted my grandfather the most. He married her in Gandharva style, which meant that there were no human witnesses; only ethereal spirits witnessed the marriage. Many are the girls who lost their virginity in this manner and left to fend for themselves. My grandfather was of a different mettle. He took his bride back home. When he reached the outskirts of the capital, he heard from some loyal troops that a coup had taken place. He quietly withdrew to avoid bloodshed and retired with his wife to a forest lodge, which was always his hide out. Then he purchased some agricultural land and became a farmer. That is how my mother was close to nature. Her father's interest in knowledge had also rubbed off on her".

"Coming to my hair, my mother told me that Grand Mother used to rub in coconut oil into her hair every day. This was supposed to promote hair growth. My mother, in turn, continued the oil rubbing routine with me. If I had a daughter, I would have continued this practice on her". Yeshua ignored the allusion and asked: "Where do you get coconut oil? I did not see any coconut palms in this area". "That is where the Southern caravan trade comes in handy. They bring coconut oil from the west coast", she replied. "My mother taught me how to filter it; otherwise it becomes rancid quickly. She also taught me how to season it with some spices. The seasoned oil is best for hair", "That must be the reason for the fragrance of your hair", observed Yeshua. "How do you know that? You hardly ever come in smelling distance of me", she shot back. "But now I can smell it", he said, snuggling closer to her and probing her hair with his hand.

"Seriously, Yeshua, even if you are going back without marrying me, why can't we have a child before you go? Give me a little Yeshua whom I can play with when you are on your mission." Yeshua replied seriously: "I believe that marriage is a contract between a man and woman to live together not only for their happiness, but also for procreation. It involves a pledge that they will have sexual relations only between the two of them. I believe that any sex outside of marriage is a sin". "That is your view" she replied. "In *Mahabharata*, Kunti had three sons from three different males, other than her husband. Why can't I have one child from the only one man I ever want to marry?" Her voice had risen to a crescendo. "You can have as many children as you want, Shaku. But only after marriage", said Yeshua, while continuing to caress her hair. "Your tea is getting cold, Yeshua", said Shakuntala and handed over his cup. As he was sipping his tea, she suddenly sat bolt upright and said: "Father has come". She quickly got up and unbolted the inner door and went to meet her father. He heard her telling her father:"Pithaji, Yeshua came home to meet you. I made some tea for him. Please talk to him while I make some tea for you also".

Acharya Sahadeva greeted Yeshua warmly, and sat down on the opposite seat. "I heard that your course on comparative religion was a roaring success. Congratulations", said Sahadeva, opening the conversation. "It was a success because of your daughter, sir", responded Yeshua. Shakuntala, who had walked into the room with a cup of tea, interjected: "Yeshua is being modest as usual. I played only a minor role". She handed over the cup to her father and sat down beside him. "He had a meeting with Acharya Shantideva today. We were discussing what transpired between the two of them". "Then tell me what happened" asked Sahadeva. Yeshua replied:"I asked the Guru whether I can go back to Palestine to pursue my mission, but he would like me to stay for one more year. Finally, the Guru gave me one week to think it over". "Then why don't you accept Shantideva's suggestion? After all it is only one year", opined Sahadeva. "Messages I am getting from Palestine say that now is the right time to launch my mission", replied Yeshua. "Pithaji, he says he is going on a dangerous mission which may even cost him his life. Please stop him from this suicide mission. Please persuade him to marry me and settle down here in Taxila. That way we can continue the Course which is something I have been looking forward to", interjected Shakuntala. "There is nothing I would like better, Shaku. I will not lose my daughter, but will gain a son, that too a brilliant son. But I know that for Yeshua, his mission is an all consuming passion, and it is a noble one. He has to make up his own mind", was Shadeva's response.

Guru Sahadeva turned to Yeshua and asked him what it was that he learned in Taxila University which would prove to be useful in his Mission to the Jews. Yeshua thought for a few moments and replied: "Guruji, I came here with a number of questions in my mind regarding God and theology and found my answers here. First of all, learning Buddhism in its most prominent seat of knowledge itself was an overwhelming experience. I am all the more happy that I had the benefit of a great scholar like Acharya Shantideva as my guide. Secondly, I learned a lot from Shakuntala. She taught me Pali, Sanskrit and Hinduism". "But you cannot use them in Palestine. My question is how the ten years that you spent in Taxila would be useful in your mission back home?" interjected Sahadeva. Yeshua replied without hesitation: "I got a much better understanding of God and religion. In essence all religions are trying to understand how the entire system works, and evolve appropriate guidelines by which people can live their lives and improve their interpersonal relationships. Each religion has its own rituals which are different from those of the others. In my opinion these differences in rituals do not matter. In fundamentals, however, we have much to learn from each other. I am not going back to Palestine to convert Jews into Buddhists or Hindus. I would like to enrich

Judaism by adding some of the lessons I have learned here form the two great religions that I had the opportunity to study." "May I ask you, for my own knowledge, what these lessons are? You can be very brief in your answer" asked the Guru. "Yes, Sir," responded Yeshua. "Both these religions have their own prescriptions on how a follower can discipline his life for the best ultimate benefits for himself and for the society as a whole. Their prescriptions are surprisingly similar – eschew greed, lust, anger and arrogance. I hope I will be successful in propagating this message while I try to reinterpret Judaism". "I wish you success in your mission, Yeshua" said the Guru. "Your message and your ability to express it so lucidly and succinctly show that the years you spent here have been worthwhile. I have one last question. "What about Shakuntala who has fallen in love with you and is determined to marry you?" Yeshua replied coolly: "Sir, my only regret in going on my mission is that I have to leave Shakuntala behind. She has been my guide, friend and philosopher all these years. I fully reciprocate her love and affection. If I can complete my mission and return, I will marry her. Believe me there is no other woman I will ever marry. But I will not marry her and leave her behind. That is not what marriage is about." "These are noble thoughts and your mission is also noble. I can only wish you success", replied the Guru, who got up and blessed Yeshua by placing both his hands on his head. The Jewish scholar sought his permission to leave, which was granted.

Shakuntala accompanied him to open the door for him. Suddenly an idea came to her mind like a flash of lightning. "Yeshua", she said, "let us plan a celebration of the success of our Course on Comparative Religiion". "We will organise a party with lunch or refreshments. We can call the entire faculty of the School of Religion", replied Yeshua. Shakuntala looked unhappy about his proposal. She said: "I was thinking of a party for just the two of us. Let us go on a picnic". Yeshua said that he was agreeable, but did not know where to go and how to provide for food. "Those details you leave to me. You just come here early tomorrow morning and go with me to a wonderful spot on Margala hills. As it is springtime, the whole place is in bloom", she suggested. After seeing off Yeshua, she called her maid Maya and gave instructions on the preparations.

When Yeshua reached Shakuntala's place early next morning, she was ready. She was dressed for the occasion in a colourful outfit. She was wearing what looked like a pleated black skirt, which was in reality a pleated piece of cotton wrapped around her waist and secured in place by means of clothe bands. This 'skirt' came down well below her knees, but gave her enough freedom of movement to climb the hill. Above the skirt she had a white breast band, which was sufficiently broad to cover her torso. It was secured in place by means of pins at the back. On top of this she had an *uttariya* (shawl) which she wrapped around her shoulders. It was made of thin silk material, light yellow in colour, with golden borders. Her wheat coloured skin shone through her *uttariya*. Her hair was plaited in two branches with each plait terminated in a ribbon knot. *This girl looks beautiful in any outfit*, thought Yeshua. He himself was wearing a cotton cloth wrapped around his waist, the front ends pulled back and tucked into the waistband. This made his legs free to walk or run. His torso was covered with an armless woven tunic. Shakuntala was carrying a basket, obviously packed with goodies for the picnic. Yeshua wanted to carry it for her, but she refused to give it. "Our lunch is already on the way. This basket contains only a few snacks", she explained. "Who is carrying the lunch?" asked Yeshua. "I will tell this on our way, because it is a long story", she explained.

As they walked towards the hill, Shakuntala told the story. "The hill and the forest on it belong to *adivasies,* which means original inhabitants. They live a primitive life compared to our standards, but they have their own social systems and customs. My grandmother had a deep interest in such communities, probably because she grew up in a hermitage and her playmates were *adivasies*. She wanted to ensure that our culture and our Government would leave them alone. In order to minimize cultural infiltration, she opposed hiring of domestic help from among the *adivasies*. She spent a lot of time studying the culture and system of *adivasy* societies. In fact, she could be considered an authority on the life styles and customs of *adivasies*. In one of her visits she heard that a couple has disappeared in a hunting expedition, leaving a three year old girl behind, As nobody came forward to adopt the child, there was a problem of bringing up the little child. My grandmother took the responsibility of bringing up the child. That is how Mayavathy came to our house, and became my playmate. My mother shortened her name to Maya. As she grew up, she started helping in household chores. When I went to school, she wanted to come with me, but that was not possible, because she was a couple of years younger than me. She went to school later and gave up studies after primary school. After leaving school she took interest in my needs like picking my dress for the day, washing and cleaning everything I used and playing with me. After my grandmother's death, my mother took charge of her and let her attend to me. After my mother passed away, I was officially in charge of her, but the fact is that she is in charge of everything in our house including kitchen, clothes and cleanliness. When I told her about this picnic yesterday evening, she decided to pack all the food and come with us. I suggested that she go earlier with the lunch and set it up. Frankly I wanted that the two of us should be alone, without any distraction."

As they started at the climb on the narrow and uneven path winding its way between trees and plants, Shakuntala held firmly on Yeshua's arm, and he in turn put a protective arm around her shoulder. When the climb was steep, Yeshua went ahead and pulled her up. When they had to cross a stream, Yeshua carried her across. A little later, she sat down to extricate a small stone that got caught between her toes and her sandals. When she got up she was limping. When Yeshua offered to carry her, she pointed out that carrying her would only weaken him, thus slowing down their progress. She suggested that instead Yeshua should put his arm around her waist and help her walk. This is how they continued their upward journey. Yeshua found it a pleasant experience to have this pretty girl in such close proximity. He now understood the logic of sending Maya ahead. Yeshua asked: "Does Maya know her way around this place? Is she not afraid of wild animals?" asked Yeshua. Shakuntala: "She has been coming here once a month to spend a couple of days with her relatives and friends. Thus she is familiar not only with the terrain, but also the people."

They reached the top region of the hills, and came to a clearing, where the trees have been cut and only a few shrubs remained. As they were looking for a place to settle down for the picnic, something attracted Yeshua's attention. A wild boar was charging towards them. He asked Shakuntala to stay behind him, while he prepared to face the beast. He had no weapon of any sort, nor was he skilled in combat; further he was against violence of any sort. In the split second available to him, he decided to use Buddhist principles. He assumed a calm and serene posture, and looked at the charging boar with love and compassion. To his surprise and relief the animal slowed down, and approached him slowly. When it reached Yeshua, it folded its haunches and sat down in a prostrated posture. Now about two dozen tribal youth, who were obviously chasing the beast, came running but they also came to a sudden halt on seeing the prostrate position of the wild beast. "Devar, Devar", shouted somebody, and the whole group chanted it in unison. "They are saying that you are god", explained Shakuntala. Hearing the chanting, about thirty young women came running from different directions and joined the party. The young men drove away the boar and made a circle around Yeshua and Shakuntala. They moved rhythmically, to the beat of a drum, in clockwise direction continuing the chant. The young women also moved in a circle, but it was a bigger circle which was rotating in the anti-clockwise direction. They were chanting 'Siva-Parvati'. The men also joined in the Siva-Parvati' chant. Together the two groups demanded the enactment of *Shiva-Parvati Swayamvara.*

Maya now appeared from nowhere and went to Shakuntala and informed her that the whole tribal community is agog with the news that Shiva and Parvathi had chosen their hill for a visit and they were going to reenact their *Swayamvara.* Maya suggested that it was better go along with their demand than to fight them. She produced two garlands and gave one each to the couple, and asked the bride to put her garland around Yeshua's neck. She promptly garlanded Yeshua and urged him follow suit, saying: "After all it is for fun". So Yeshua garlanded Shakuntala. Now there was another chant from the revelers who were enjoying their dance in circles. Maya interpreted it for the 'divine' couple. They want the couple should kiss each other. Meanwhile the rhythm became faster and the chanting became louder. Yeshua protested and said that this was a serious matter not meant for public display. Maya communicated this to the dancers, and came back with the reply that they would all look elsewhere during the kissing session. Shakuntala now said: "Come on Yeshua, what chance do we have to escape from this crowd of over fifty people, if we do not comply?. Anyway, it is not a sin to kiss the only man whom I am going to marry." After ensuring that even Maya was banished from the scene, she put her arms around Yeshua's neck and kissed him on the lips. She was pleasantly surprised to note that he responded and enjoyed their first sensuous kiss. They broke off only when they heard the loud clap from the crowd.

After these exciting events, Yeshua and Shakuntala were escorted to the Chief of the Tribe, whose words were interpreted by Maya. The Chief stood up to receive the guests and expressed his happiness over the visit of Shiva and Parvati to his tribe. He pointed out that most of the tribal people were devotees of Shiva. He sought the protection of the Lord against wild animals. His people, he said, marveled at the power of the Lord when a wild boar prostrated before him. He added that he would have been happy to prepare lunch for the divine couple, but he was told that lunch was already arranged. They were then led to a spacious hut where lunch was being set up. The visitors sat on woven grass mats topped by folded sheets that Maya had brought with her. The lunch consisting of *roti* (bread), rice, *d*ahl (lentil), vegetables and meat was served on leaves by Maya and her friends. After lunch the visiting couple was given a guided tour of the forest by the same group. They saw a typical *adivasy* hut, which could be dismantled and carried to another location easily. Maya showed them the different berries that adorned the trees of the forest. "Not all of them are edible", Maya pointed out. "Some are bitter and some are even poisonous. But most of them are delicious; they are god's gift to the tribals. Because of that no tribal goes to sleep hungry". Yeshua and Parvati tried some of them and certified that they were indeed delicious. After walking around for a couple of hours, they felt hungry and sat down to eat the refreshments brought by Shakuntala. Then it was time to go home. This time Maya walked with them to show them the way, especially the short cuts, so that they could get out of the forest before it got dark. She whispered in her playmate's ear: "I will walk ahead so that you can do your mischief with your man, who looks very innocent". Shakuntala pinched her and whispered back: "You come home and I will give my reply. Now you run along". Shakuntala took hold of Yeshua's hand and walked downhill, supported by her beau.

By the time they reached Shakuntala's house, it was already dark. She asked her escort whether he enjoyed the picnic. "Of course, I enjoyed it thoroughly, especially your company. But I cannot help feeling that the show at the clearing was stage managed". "I swear to you that I did not do any stage managing. If Maya or her tribal friends did it, I am not responsible". Yeshua responded: "I am still curious to find out how they did it. Shall we call Maya and find out?" "Of course you can find out for yourself", was the reply. She went inside the house and came back with Maya. Yeshua asked: "Tell me Maya, how did you organise the show involving the boar and the young men as well as women of Margala Hills?" Maya said: "I did not make any prior arrangement, as Shakuntala told me about the picnic only yesterday evening. When I went there, I told some of my brothers and sisters that the *Shiva-Parvathi* couple were coming on a visit and if they can be made to reenact their *Swayamvara*, it would be fun. I did not even know about the wild boar. Even now I think that it was Yeshua's calm and compassionate approach that pacified the boar. I have heard it said by the tribal hunters that wild animals recognise divine personalities. That is why they never attack Rishis and Sages". She sought and obtained permission to leave. Shakuntala turned to Yeshua and said: "Are you satisfied now? Even if you suspect I stage managed it, I have no regrets. Do you know how Parvati won over Shiva?" Yeshua told her he did not know, because he was rather poor in Hindu mythology. "Then I will tell you", she said. "From her childhood Parvati was a devotee of Shiva. As she grew up, it became love, and she wanted to marry only Lord Shiva. Because of her beauty and intelligence, many marriage proposals came to her, but she rejected them all. Finally, her father took her to Lord Shiva and requested him to allow her to help him in his *puja*. Shiva agreed, but did not even look at her. She decided to do a penance to win over Shiva, who lived an ascetic life and concentrated only on *puja*. The penance was so intense that she did not eat or drink and was not even aware of her environment. Many sages came to visit her on hearing about the intensity of her penance. Finally Shiva himself came in the form of a priest to test her. Finding her steadfast devotion and indomitable determination, Shiva identified himself and agreed to marry her. She told him that he should approach her father and ask for her hand in marriage. Lord Shiva complied and that is how they were united in marriage. That is the power of a woman's determination".

She continued: "In my case, I have over fifty witnesses who will certify that we are married to each other in a *Swayamvara* ceremony. The same witnesses will also testify that we engaged in a post nuptial kiss. It is the first time I kissed a man and he is the man I have implanted in my heart as my husband". Yeshua told her: "Shakuntala, you don't need witnesses to prove that we exchanged garlands in a reenactment of Shiva-Parvati marriage and that we kissed each other. For me also it was a first romantic kiss, and I must say I liked it. I also want to assure you that if I ever marry, you will be my bride. The only obstacle is my mission which is my first priority. I realise that there some elements of risk in my mission. If I survive them, I will definitely come back to marry you. But I am not putting you under any obligation to wait for me". "You stupid man, haven't you understood what I said? I have already enshrined you in my heart. Whether you come back or not, you and only you will always be there. If we are agreed on that, give me one more kiss to affirm our pact". Yeshua held her in a tight embrace and kissed her, saying:"Shaku, you are the only woman whom I have ever kissed with passion in all my life and I assure you that I will not even look at another with desire in my mind until the end of my days."I believe you Yeshua, for I know that you tell only the truth" she replied. They remained locked in embrace for a long time. Finally, he extricated himself and slowly walked back to his room.

CHAPTER 7

Earthquake and Return to Palestine

Yeshua was sitting in his room pondering over the events of the past few days. It all started with a message he received from Yohan, which said that things were coming to the boiling point in Palestine. In his view, the time was ripe for Yeshua to return and start his work. Yohan also stated that Yeshua's parents, Miriam and Yosef, were anxious to meet their son after more than ten years. How quickly the years have passed, thought Yeshua. He could vividly recall arriving at Taxila with Yosef of Arimathea, and meeting King Gondophares in his palace at Sirkap. How many people have helped him over the past ten years! Yosef introduced him to the King, who recommended him for the post of AramaicTeacher. Guru Sahadeva selected him for this post. Shakuntala taught him Pali in her spare time. Guru Shantideva gave him admission in the School of Religion and recommended him for the King's scholarship. Several teachers in this School taught him. Physician Sanjeevan was extremely helpful throughout the period he spent in Medical School. The course in Comparative Religion was so successful because of Shakuntala and all the members of the School of Religion. He felt sad that he had to leave Shakuntala behind and go away.

As he sat in his chair pondering over these issues, Yeshua heard a roaring noise and felt that his chair was being pulled back from behind him. It took a few seconds to realise that he had just experienced an earth quake. He ran outside to find that many people had already come out. There was no heavy damage in the School of Religion, as the buildings were of low profile, built with clay bricks and thatched roofs. Yeshua recollected that the School of Languages was housed in more modern buildings made of large stones and tiled roofs. He ran over there to ascertain whether Shakuntala and her father were safe. Part of the main building had collapsed. The Guru's residence had also partially collapsed. Yeshua went over there to find Guru Sahadeva crushed under a fallen stone with Shakuntala weeping unabashedly. She kept repeating: "Why was I spared? I would have gladly taken his place. Pithaji was a great asset to this university". Yeshua took the help of some students and extricated Sahadeva from under the stone and realised that the Guru was badly injured, but was alive. They carried him over to the hospital, where he got the best medical care possible. He went to hospital store and secured a packet of narcotic powder, which he dissolved in a tumbler of water and gave to Shakuntala to calm her nerves and put her to sleep. She kept on asking about the condition of her father. Yeshua told her that the doctors were attending to him and they were hopeful of saving him. Gradually Shakuntala dozed off to sleep. He then left her under the care of her maid servant and some girls from the dormitory. He ran to the hospital and found that Guru Sahadeva's condition was critical. A few hours later he was pronounced dead. Yeshua knew that Sahadeva was an advocate of cremation; so was his daughter. So he made arrangements for cremation before sunset, and decided to wake up Shakuntala only an hour before that.

Most students and faculty were gathered at the cremation ground. The body of Guru Sahadeva was laid on a makeshift platform of sandalwood beams, covered with flowers showered on him by the students. When Shakuntala came, accompanied by Yeshua and members of the School of Languages, the crowd parted, making room for Shakuntala to reach her father's body. She practically fell on the body, weeping inconsolably. She kept repeating: "Why did this happen? What harm has my father done to anyone? He was such a good man, the only relative I had in this world". Yeshua tried to console her by saying that it was the effect of an earth quake, which unfortunately hit her house. But she was not even listening. She suddenly turned to him and asked: "Yeshua, can I at least light my father's pyre? I am his only relative". Yeshua consulted Guru Shantideva, who said: "There is no rule against it, though it is usually done by male heirs. I am for allowing her to perform the last rites". Thus Shakuntala lit the pyre, with tears flowing down her cheeks in copious quantities. Yeshua then led her back to her house, and gave her another drink to let her sleep peacefully. Leaving her with some female volunteers, Yeshua walked back to his room. It was late at night when he hit his bed.

Though he had heard that Sirkap was badly hit by the earth quake, he could go there only on the second day, as he was very busy on the first day taking care of Shakuntala and her father. He saw that most buildings in the capital were damaged. This could be attributed to their granite block construction. The Palace was badly hit. He soon found out that King Gondophares himself was killed and was interred with State honours. The Capital was in mourning for the beloved King. Yeshua recalled his visit to the palace with Yosef of Arimathea. The King was gracious and kind. In fact, it was he who suggested the possibility of Yeshua teaching Aramaic to the traders to earn a living at the beginning of his studies. He later sanctioned a Royal scholarship for Yeshua's regular study in the University. He noticed that the Army had taken the job of clearing the debris and distributing food and medicines. The Royal physicians and nurses were attending to those who were hurt in the earth quake. As he could not contribute anything to Sirkap, Yeshua went to meet Acharya Shantideva to seek his counsel. The Guru gave him the latest news. The indication from the Palace was that the King's son would succeed him, assuming the name Gondophares II. It was a well known fact that the new king was not supportive of the University. Moreover, funds had to be found for rebuilding Sirkap. Therefore, it was unlikely that new posts or scholarships would get sanctioned. Shantideva felt that he could take care of Shakuntala by down grading the post of Sahadeva and offering it to her. This would also make sure that she could continue to stay in the present house. The University had already started repair of the house. It was fortunate that Yeshua wanted to return to his native land, as no position could be offered to him.

Yeshua went over to Shakuntala's place and told her what he heard from Guru Shantideva. "So you have decided to leave me alone and go back?" she exclaimed. Yeshua reminded her that this was the decision that was taken with the blessings of her father. She said: "At least stay on for a few days, until I come to terms with my predicament."Of course, I will do that. In fact, I can leave only when the caravan comes and returns. That may take at least a month". Shakuntala wanted Yeshua to stay with her during that period. But he ruled it out as improper. He agreed to spend the day time with her to do all the necessary chores, but he spent the nights in his room. After about three weeks, he got a message from Yosef of Arimathea announcing his arrival. Yosef had brought messages from Yohan as well as Yeshua's parents. Yohan urged him to return immediately as the time was just right. Yosef and Miriam expressed their eagerness to see their son. Yosef of Arimathea asked Yeshua to accompany him when he made the courtesy call on the new King. The King received Yosef, accepted his gifts and assured Yosef that he could expect to get all assistance with the caravan, "Trade is our life blood", he added. He turned to Yeshua and said: "I have heard about you and know that the University holds you in high regard, Our financial position does not permit any addition to the strength of the university, so we are unable extend an invitation to you to join the faculty. It may be possible to do this at a future date". "Yeshua has already decided to go back to his people to lead them in fulfilling their covenant with God", interjected Yosef. "That sounds like a noble cause. Wish you good luck, young man", said the King.

Two weeks later, Yeshua joined the caravan to return to Palestine. Shakuntala made it clear to him that she expected him to come back to marry her and take her with him wherever he decided to settle down. However, she packed a medicine box full of Ayurvedic medicines picked up from the School of Medicine, with each individual packet labelled carefully along with a note on its application and risks. The return journey was a lot more comfortable for Yeshua than his inward journey. For example, he travelled with Yosef of Arimathea in the coach, reflecting his new status. The food served was better, and facilities provided at stopovers were superior. In spite of this, Yeshua was frequently seen with young employees and volunteers. He was also helpful at border check posts. The journey still took several weeks. They went up the Oxus Valley and Yeshua enjoyed the crisp mountain air. It was also a great pleasure to take a dip in the clear waters of the mountain river. At Bactra, the caravan party took a break for a couple of days. Many people in Bactra had heard about the earthquake in Taxila and the death of King Gondophares, who was obviously very popular. All the questions about the earthquake and the King were directed to Yeshua, not only because of his proficiency in the local language but also because he actually experienced the earth quake. Yeshua was touched by the concern shown by total strangers for the victims of the earthquake and the great regard for the late King.

Yeshua preferred to sleep in the open during the break at Bactra. As he gazed at the clear sky, he recognised the familiar constellations. He soon found that he was not alone. Two Essene riders of the caravan were sent by Yosef of Arimathea to keep him company. The youngsters were keen to learn about stars and their constellations. "Which is that star", asked one of the Essenes, pointing at Venus which was rising in the east. Yeshua explained to him that Venus was probably not a star, as it did not have its own light. Half the year it trails the setting sun, thus making itself visible through reflected light, and in the other half of the year it appears ahead of the rising sun. Seeing the puzzled look of his companions, he explained it further. "Even though the sun has set for us", he pointed out, "Venus is in sight of the sun and is just reflecting the light from the sun. If we wait for some time, Venus will not be visible, as its reflected rays cannot reach us". He could teach the youngsters about the Big Dipper, the constellation with seven stars, known in India as *saptarishies* [seven saints]. He explained how the sailors located the pole star which gave them the north direction. They draw an imaginary line joining the two outer stars of the Big Dipper, and keep extrapolating it until the line reaches the pole star. Orion, also known as the Celestial Hunter, was another constellation which attracted the attention of the Essenes. Yeshua pointed out the arrow of the hunter, his head and feet and his belt. He noted that the three stars which made up the belt were among the brighter stars of the firmament, suggesting that Orion was closer to us than most stars. Yeshua told his companions that, looking at the sky, he understood how David the shepherd was inspired to write his famous Psalm 19, which all of them recited together.

Psalm 19

The heavens declare the glory of God; and the firmament shows his handiwork.

Day unto day utters speech, and night unto night shows knowledge.

There is no speech nor language, where their voice is not heard.

Their line is gone out through all the earth, and their words to the end of the world. In them hath he set a tabernacle for the sun,

Which is as a bridegroom coming out of his chamber, and rejoices as a strong man to run a race.

His going forth is from the end of the heaven, and his circuit unto the ends of it: and there is nothing hid from the heat thereof.

The law of the LORD is perfect, comforting the soul: the testimony of the LORD is sure, making wise the simple.

The statutes of the LORD are right, rejoicing the heart: the commandment of the LORD is pure, enlightening the eyes.

The fear of the LORD is clean, enduring for ever: the judgments of the LORD are true and righteous altogether.

More to be desired are they than gold, yea, than much fine gold: sweeter also than honey and the honeycomb.

Moreover by them is thy servant warned: and in keeping of them there is great reward.

Who can understand his errors? Cleanse thou me from secret faults.

Keep back thy servant also from presumptuous sins; let them not have dominion over me: then shall I be upright, and I shall be innocent from the great transgression.

Let the words of my mouth, and the meditation of my heart, be acceptable in thy sight, O LORD, my strength, and my redeemer.

Yeshua was quite happy when the caravan crossed the border into Parthia where Aramaic was the official language. He had no problem conversing with the officials at the border and even shop keepers. He persuaded Yosef of Arimathea to give an extra break at Ctesiphon-Seleucia so that he could walk around and see the large Greek city of Seleucia and the Parthian capital Ctesiphon, which was used by the Parthian rulers at least in winter. He observed that the houses in Ctesiphon were larger and more luxurious than those in Seleucia, obviously because the royalty and high ranking officials lived there. He marvelled at the sight of Tigris River, but had to concede that Indus was bigger is size and volume of water, being fed by the ice caps of the Himalayas. He told his friends that if there was time, he would have gone and visited historically important places like Babylon, where the Jews were taken and held in captivity by Nebuchadnezzar, and Nineveh which was the capital the of Assyrian Empire and its ruler Sennacherib who ransacked Samaria and deported its citizens to the eastern parts of the Empire. Yeshua's knowledge of history and his enthusiasm to visit historical places impressed his friends and fellow travellers.

They now moved faster along the plains. When the caravan reached Damascus, Yosef decided to break off from the caravan and take his coach along with his distinguished guest directly to Jerusalem, accompanied only by a couple of security guards on horseback. The rest of the caravan proceeded to Antioch and beyond under the supervision of his senior colleagues. This bifurcation made it possible for Yosef to make a small detour to Nazareth and drop off Yeshua at his door step. Yeshua felt embarrassed at this generosity, but his parents were thrilled. For many months, Miriam would tell her neighbours that Yosef of Arimathea personally brought her son home. "You should have seen the coach and the horses. So magnificent", she boasted.

It was like festival time in their house. Neighbours and relatives dropped in to see Yeshua who had returned after higher studies abroad. They were all treated to tasty food prepared by Miriam, who was glowing in the reflected glory. She herself pointed out that Yeshua had reached the age for priesthood. There was also a hint that marriage proposals were welcome. "Now you will look for proposals only from some wealthy family", quipped some of the relatives. Early next week, Yohan came over to visit his cousin. "Where were you all thus time, Yohan? Why did it take you so long to get here?" asked Miriam, ushering him in. "I came to know of his arrival only yesterday, Aunty", replied Yohan.

CHAPTER 8

Mission to the Jews

Early next morning, the two cousins went for a long walk to their favourite spot on the south western corner of the Sea of Galilee. First of all, Yohan wanted to hear about Yeshua's sojourn and all that he learned in Taxila. So Yeshua told him about his caravan trip to Taxila, his studies at Taxila University, the courses he attended, the course he conducted on comparative religion, the earth quake and his return trip. He did not forget to mention the role of Yosef of Arimathea. "You are indeed the Messiah that we have been waiting for. I have made a plan for launching your mission. We plan to do that during the wedding at Cana to which you will be invited. It will be an occasion for people to know you. I will tell you the details later", said Yohan. Yeshua then enquired about Yohan and the Essene Movement. Yohan told his cousin that he had become an Elder. In fact, he became an Elder as soon he reached the age of thirty in the previous year. He added: "As I told you earlier, Elders have to perform priestly duties. As prescribed in the scriptures, you can become a priest only if you are thirty. So it is with Elders. Now-a-days I am baptising people in River Jordan". Yeshua raised his eyebrows and said: "I thought that baptism was not necessary for those who are circumcised. Circumcision is the covenant". "Scripturally speaking, you are right. But there is no harm in making an affirmation when you come of age. Let me add that, as far as we are concerned, this is also an admission to our movement. You must come and see the line up for baptism", answered Yohan. "I will certainly come", assured Yeshua.

On Sabbath Day, Yeshua accompanied the rest of the family to the synagogue. He was asked to read the scripture and explain it. He opened the Book of Isaiah and read the verses which said: "The Spirit of The Lord is on me, because the Lord has anointed me to preach good news to the poor. He has sent me to heal the broken hearted, to proclaim freedom for the captives, to give release from darkness for the prisoners, to proclaim the year of Lord's favour, and to comfort those who grieve". By way of interpretation, he said: "Though this was written at a time when Israel was threatened by their enemies, it is very relevant in the current time. For the Kingdom of God is at hand. We must prepare ourselves to receive it. This is our mission. There are amongst us many who are poor, broken hearted, and sick. It is our duty to minister unto them. We have to give a healing touch to those who suffer from illnesses and comfort those who are in grief from bereavement or personal problems. When the Kingdom of God is established, we are accountable only to God almighty and not to any foreign power". The whole congregation marvelled at his words and the authority with which he spoke. Many people came and congratulated Miriam for bringing up such an erudite son. She was very pleased to hear such wholesome praise.

Early next week Yeshua went to River Jordan to see for himself how Yohan baptised those who came to him. There was a line of people waiting to be baptised Yeshua joined the queue. Only when he reached Yohan did the baptist recognise the next person in line. He said: "You are the Messiah. How can I baptise you?". Yeshua pointed out that he had come to show solidarity with the Essene Movement, and therefore he should be baptised. So Yohan baptised him. As Yeshua waded to the River bank, Yohan told those who were waiting that he had just baptised the Messiah. "How do you know", asked them. Yohan said: "I felt that Holy Spirit had come down in the form of a dove and hovered over his head". He called two of his disciples to follow Yeshua and show him the house he had arranged for him to stay when he started his mission. Yeshua found the modest dwelling adequate for his immediate use. The disciples, named Andrew and Philip, told him that they would like to join him in his mission and follow him. Yeshua told them that they were welcome to join him, but they had to wait for a few days, as immediately he wanted to spend some time in meditation in the wilderness. "What about your food, when you are in the wilderness?" they asked. "I can survive with very little food during meditation. Moreover, the wilderness is full of food. It is said that Yohan spends a lot of time in the wilderness and survives on locusts and honey" replied Yeshua.

The focus of his meditation was his mission - how to go about achieving his goals. He pondered over several options. One possibility was to perform miracles to solve people's problems like providing food and healing the sick. While food and healing were necessary, the miracle route was neither practical nor honest, and hence it was rejected. Capturing political power through armed struggle was a potential option, but that has never worked, as was demonstrated by the most recent efforts of the Macabees. The only route to political power was to make a deal with Roman masters and rule like Herod. This option was unacceptable, and therefore ruled out. The third option was to take over the Jewish leadership. The quick route to this was to make a deal with the priests, after a campaign to win over popular support. But in any such deal, the priestly class would extract many benefits which would be inconsistent with his objectives. *All these were just temptations*, Yeshua reminded himself. His real calling was teaching the people about God and making them understand his real nature. The message of the scripture would have to be reinterpreted towards this end. Thus at the end of the meditations in the wilderness, Yeshua came back with a clear vision of his mission and the methodology to be used. He had as his capital everything that he learned in Rabbi Gamaliel's academy and at Taxila University. Intellectual understanding is even more important than emotional loyalty, he told himself. When he came back from his meditation, his disciples, Andrew and Philip, were waiting for him. There was a third person whom Andrew introduced as his brother Simon, who was keen to be a disciple. Yeshua welcomed him and said: "You will now be known as Peter, the rock". After Peter's induction, Yeshua went to Nazareth to spend a few days with his family.

Miriam told Yeshua about the wedding at Cana, where her cousin's daughter was getting married. The whole family was invited, especially Yeshua. Thus Yeshua went with his parents and brothers to Cana. As the feast was going on, he came out and loitered around. Then he saw his mother walking briskly towards him. She asked: "Son, they have run out of wine. Please do something". "Mother, you should know that I do not approve of these drunken revelries. Ask them to drink water", Yeshua replied. Miriam asked him to do what he can. Then she turned to a few youngsters standing there and told them: "You do whatever he asks you to do". The youngsters went to Yeshua and asked him what they should do. Yeshua told them to fill up the stone cisterns with water and serve it as wine. The youngsters were Essene volunteers sent by Yohan. They filled up the cisterns with the wine they had brought with them, and gave it to be served. The wine taster went to the host and asked: "Why are you serving such good wine at the end? Normally it is done the other way - strong wine is served first". News spread fast that Yeshua had turned water into wine. As the family was walking back to Nazareth, Miriam told Yeshua: "That was a remarkable miracle that you performed". "I did not perform any miracle", Yeshua affirmed. The rest of the group exchanged knowing glances.

Yeshua felt that in the Nazareth area, he would always be thought of as son of Yosef and Miriam. He recalled the statement that no prophet was honoured in his native place. So he moved his operations to the northern banks of the Sea of Galilee, and chose the towns of Capernaum and Bethsaida for his immediate mission. There he was well received in the synagogues where he preached. Seeing the sick people who came near the synagogues on the Sabbath day, he decided that healing should be an important component of his mission. Many in that group, either directly or through their relatives who brought them here, claimed that they were possessed by evil spirits. Yeshua used the hypnosis technique that he used with great success in Taxila. He hypnotised the patient nearest to him and found out that the 'evil spirit' was none other than a local rowdy who met with a violent death. With great authority, he asked the evil spirit to leave the patient alone. The patient woke up as if from a dream, and thanked Yeshua for his healing. He healed a few more people and moved on for the day. His fame spread ahead of him, and wherever he went big crowds followed him. When he was preaching to a group of people on the banks of Lake Galilee at Bethsaida, the crowd increased rapidly, forcing him to move to the edge of the lake. He beckoned to a fishing boat which was standing nearby. Going aboard, he continued his sermon from his perch on the boat. Only when he finished did he realise that the boat belonged to Simon Peter and his brother Andrew. He asked them: "Where is your catch?" Peter answered: "Master, we were fishing all night, but could not catch any fish?" Yeshua said: "Then cast your net on the right side of the boat". They did so, and caught a net full of fish. Peter called his partners in the neighbouring boat to help. The owners of the second boat, James and John, known as sons of Zebedee, also became Yeshua's disciples. Gradually seven others joined as disciples, namely Bartholomew, Mathew, Thomas, James the son of Alphaeus, Jude also known as Thaddeus, Simon the Zealot, and Judas Iscariot. The total number of disciples became twelve.

Yeshua noticed that several people who were seeking cure were afflicted with blindness. A closer examination showed that some of them were suffering from an eye infection. This he knew could be cured by an Ayurvedic medicine that he brought with him from Taxila. Some others became blind as a result of some psychosomatic problems. They could be cured by hypnosis followed by powerful suggestion, amounting to an order. This he would do in the name of God. He knew that he was helpless in the case of congenial blindness. In the next visit to the synagogue, he carried with him the appropriate Ayurvedic powder. On examination of some blind men, he found a case of infection. He took out some powder [some onlookers thought it was dust] and made a paste with water and applied it on the man's eyes, and asked him to go to the Sea of Galilee and wash it off. His disciples asked Yeshua why the blind man was sent on a long walk to the Sea of Galilee, while there were other water bodies available nearby. He told them that the medicine he applied needed some time to act. Most probably, the man would come back with partial sight. He may need a couple of sessions before he regained full vision. He also cast out many evil spirits, ordering them to leave 'in the name of 'God, my Father in Heaven'. His fame spread rapidly, and his healing mission contributed a lot to his popularity.

Gradually, Yeshua moved his operation to the left bank of Jordan, especially Decapolis and Perea. This was mainly because of the advice of Yohan, whose Essene work was in this region. Yohan the Baptist, as he came to be known, was *persona non grata* for Herod Antipas, because Yohan criticised him for marrying the wife of his brother Philip. Huge crowds attended Yeshua's meetings. Initially, crowd management by Essene volunteers helped, but soon they came in big numbers on their own. Some came to get cure for their illnesses. Yeshua's main theme was that the Kingdom of God was at hand. This Kingdom was one in which God's values, namely righteousness, and compassion, prevailed. "If you are low in spirit", he said, take heart because the Kingdom of God is here. "Those who mourn should feel happy, because they will be comforted. Those who are meek will inherit the earth in the new

Kingdom. Those who hunger and thirst after righteousness, have reason to be happy, for they will find their goal. Those who are merciful will get mercy. The pure in heart should rejoice, for they will see God. The peacemakers are blessed, for they will be called the children of God. Those who are persecuted for the sake of righteousness should rejoice, for theirs is the Kingdom of God". The picture he painted was that of a place of peace and tranquillity, where "the wolf and the lamb shall dwell together, and the leopard shall lie down with the kid; the calf and the young lion and the falling together; and a little child shall lead them", as prophesied by Isaiah. He also exhorted his followers that they were the salt of the earth. They should remember what happens when salt loses its saltiness. Drawing on another analogy, he likened them to the light that shines in the Kingdom. The purpose of light was to dispel darkness. Therefore, light should be put on a pedestal rather than kept hidden under an inverted bushel.

Yeshua asserted that he wanted to fulfil the Law, rather than to disrupt it. He reinterpreted the Law, extending and adding a good measure of compassion which he held was a great virtue. He said: "The Law says that thou shall not kill. I say that you should eschew all forms of violence. The Law says that thou shall not commit adultery. I say that if you look at a woman with lust in your mind, you have already committed adultery. It is lust that has to be eliminated. The Law says that you should love your neighbour, but permits you to hate your enemy. But I say unto you that you should love even your enemy. Being angry without reason is a sin. When you go to the altar to make an offering and at the last moment remember that your brother has a problem with you, you must first go and make up with your brother, and only after that make the offering. Nonviolence is the hallmark of the Kingdom. If somebody hits you on one cheek, show him the other cheek also. If somebody forces you walk a mile with him, go an extra mile. Greed is another evil that controls human behaviour. It prompts people to accumulate wealth - whether it is storing grain in their barns, or acquiring property in the form of land, mansions and ornaments. This causes anxieties to multiply. On the other hand, you look at the birds of the sky. They need only their daily food in the form of grain left behind by the reapers. They have no accumulated wealth, nor any anxieties. When you look at the people who control our community, namely the priests and the Pharisees, we see a lot of arrogance and hypocrisy. Arrogance is a sin along with lust, anger or rage, and greed, which eat away your vitals."

"Hypocrisy is associated with arrogance. It is public posturing with no internal basis. For example, when the Pharisees fast, they put on a big show with long faces. The person who is on a genuine fast does not show it in his appearance. It is also obvious in the way they pray. They pray in a loud voice and in public places so that they are noticed by others. Real prayer is meditation. When you pray you should get into your chamber, close the door and pray in silence to your Father in Heaven. Even though others don't hear you, God can hear you. When you pray, do not go for long winding prayers as the Pharisees do. Make it short, because God can read what is in your heart even before you have spelt it out. I suggest a short prayer like this. "Our Father, who is in Heaven, hallowed be Thy name. May Thy Kingdom come and Thy will be done on earth, just as it is in Heaven. Give us this day our daily bread. Forgive us our trespasses, as we forgive them that trespass against us. Lead us not into temptation, and deliver us from evil". We should strive to be perfect, as our Father in Heaven is perfect." Yeshua recounted the story of a rich man who asked him: "What should I do to get eternal life". He was advised him to follow the Law as given in the Scripture. The rich man said that he was already doing that. "In that case", Yeshua said, "go and sell all your riches and give it to the poor." The man went away because he was too attached to his material wealth to give it away. Yeshua pointed out that those who are too attached to their possessions should not expect any rewards from God. "That is why it is said that it would be easier for a camel to go through the eye of a needle than for a rich man to enter the heavenly Kingdom."

Yeshua realised that his sermon was longer than usual, and that it was getting past lunch time. He asked the crowd: *Have you got some food to eat?* A young boy got up and said that he had brought a lunch pack of five bread cakes and two fishes. The boy then went and handed over his lunch pack to the Master. Yeshua blessed it, and asked the crowd to share their lunch with their neighbours. Meanwhile, the Essene volunteers distributed the lunch packets that they had brought. Thus the crowd had a sumptuous lunch. Soon news spread that Yeshua fed five thousand people with five bread cakes. After lunch many sick people were brought to him for healing. He concentrated on psychosomatic cases Ike those who were 'possessed with evil spirits', and the blind. Yeshua noticed that there were many cases of leprosy. He recalled that Physician Sanjeevan and colleagues in Taxila Medical School were working on a cure for leprosy. In fact, Sanjeevan had told him that they were close to announcing an Ayurvedic medicine for this illness. Yeshua sent a letter to Sanjeevan, through Yosef of Arimathya, asking him about the progress of this work, and whether it could be supplied when ready. He also expressed his readiness to pay for it through the same channel. When Yosef came back from his next caravan trip, he brought with him a large box full of Ayurvedic medicines and two letters - one from Shakuntala and the other from Sanjeevan. By way of explanation, Yosef said that he met Shakuntala to find out how she was doing, and found her adjusting to the new reality and concentrating on her work. Yeshua opened Shakuntala's letter first. She reprimanded him for not writing to her, but was happy to hear that his mission was moving forward. He should complete his mission quickly and return to Taxila; otherwise she would come to Palestine. For the present, she would wait for him. Sanjeevan's letter was more down to earth. He wrote about the package of medicines. Each one was packed with a write up and instructions for its application. He referred to the cure for leprosy, and the breakthrough they achieved. While the application of the medicine on the affected part was described in detail in the write up, he cautioned about the possibility of the physician and the assistant getting infected. He had packed in a good quantity of gloves for the care giver. He chided Yeshua for offering to pay for the medicine. "You should know that our Ayurvedic Centre never charges for medicine", he wrote.

Along with the disciples, there was a small group of women, mostly from respected families, who became part of Yeshua's entourage. Mary Magdalene was a prominent member of this group. She became a follower after Yeshua "cast out" some evil spirits from her. Yeshua noticed her dedication to the mission and willingness to do voluntary work. He decided to entrust the medicine chest to her. She was asked to study the documents about each medicine and to be prepared to apply it. From that time onwards, Mary Magdalene became the key figure in the healing mission. While Yeshua concentrated on psychosomatic cases and blindness, Mary specialised in leprosy and general diseases. Yeshua was happy to note that many lepers were getting cured, often with Mary's repeated treatment. Word went around that Yeshua cured lepers. Everywhere he went many lepers were waiting for him. Yeshua called Mary to treat them. She was meticulous in her work, and took care to protect herself from infection by wearing gloves while applying the medicine on the affected parts. After watching her for some time, Yeshua stopped worrying about her getting infected by the disease. Mary was also very popular with the patients who came for treatment. Once the lepers were cured, they were sent to the nearest priest to certify that they were cured and that they could live a normal life.

Around this time, Yeshua got the disturbing news that Yohan the Baptist was arrested and put into prison on the orders of Herod Antipas. The reason was that Yohan criticised Antipas for marrying his brother's wife. Later he got the news that Yohan was beheaded. He grieved for his cousin, friend and supporter. On digging a little deeper into the events, Yeshua found that he could be one of the causes his cousin's death. Herodias, the current wife of Antipas, had a daughter named Salome from her ex-husband, Philip. This girl used to attend Yeshua's sermons in camouflage. She was so impressed by the young Rabbi that she wanted to get closer him. As she tried to sneak into the inner circle, the Essene volunteers in charge of crowd control stopped her. On being questioned, she insisted on meeting Yeshua. The Essenes told her that she should first meet Yohan. Yohan told her that he knew who she was, and that her mother Herodias was living in sin, and refused permission. Salome went and reported to her mother. Under pressure from Herodias, the King put Yohan in prison. Salome's chance for revenge came when Herod was celebrating his birthday, and she was asked to dance in front of the royal guests. A drunken Herod liked the dance and told Salome that she could ask any gift; whatever it was, it would be granted. Salome asked for the head of the Baptist on a platter. Then Yeshua withdrew into the wilderness to silently mourn for Yohan.

Yeshua continued to preach about the Kingdom of God. His tool was the parable. A parable is a story or a natural situation, which illustrates an eternal truth. He used the parable of the sower to illustrate how his message would be received. He said: "A farmer went out to sow. A part of his grain fell by the wayside and were swallowed by the birds of the air. Some others fell on rocky ground, where they sprouted but withered when the sun came out, as they had no roots. Some fell among thorns. As the shoots sprouted, the thorns choked and killed them. Only some fell on fertile ground, which gave thirty, sixty and even hundredfold yield. The same can be said about this message. The words were heard but did not reach the mind of some listeners. Some others received the message, but the attractions of evil dominated their lives, and they forgot the message. Another group also received the message, but their own wickedness, whether it was greed, lust or deceitfulness, choked the message and did not allow it to bear fruit. There were, however, some who received the message, pondered over it and benefited from it." He likened the Kingdom of God to a mustard seed, which is the smallest seed, but when it takes root, it grows into a tree and brings forth an abundance of seeds. The idea of the Kingdom can spread likewise. Leavening of the dough is another parable that he used. A woman puts a little leaven into the dough and by next day the whole dough is leavened. So also the Kingdom of God spreads everywhere, once it is initiated.

Yeshua stressed the need for vigilance, while waiting for the arrival of the Kingdom of God. In order to explain this, he told the parable of the ten maidens, who were waiting for the arrival of the bridegroom to escort him to the inner chamber. Five of the maidens took care to stock enough oil for their lamps to last for the whole night. The other five were less prepared. All of them dozed off during the long vigil. Then there was a shout announcing the arrival of the groom. The first five picked up their lamps and escorted the groom into the inner chamber. The other five virgins found their lamps unlit, as they had gone dry. They tried to borrow oil from the others, but were refused. Similarly only those who have made sufficient preparation will be able to get into the Kingdom.

In the new dispensation, those who worked harder would be rewarded more. To illustrate this, Yeshua told the parable of the talents. A wealthy nobleman decided to go on a long trip abroad. Before going he called three of his trusted associates, and entrusted them with sufficient funds to carry on business. To the first, he gave ten talents, to the second he gave five and to the third he gave two talents. When the nobleman returned after his long sojourn, he called his associates to account. The first man came forward and said: "Master, you gave me ten talents, but I have doubled it to twenty". The second man said: "Master, you entrusted me with five talents, but I invested it and made it ten". The third man said: "Sir, I knew that you were a difficult man to please. So I kept the talent you gave me very safely, and here it is". The Master said: "You lazy man, get out of my sight". He asked his servants to throw him out, and give his talents to the one who doubled his talents to twenty. He said: "He that has doubled his talents will get more, but he that could not add to his talents, will have even his modest capital taken away from him". However, all are equal once they enter the Kingdom of God.".

Yeshua taught that it was a compassionate and forgiving God who presided over the universe. His concern for people was like that of a shepherd to his sheep. He said: "Consider a shepherd with hundred sheep in his care. At nightfall, one was found missing. Will he not leave the other 99 in the pen, and go in search of the one lost sheep? When he finds it, he will carry it back and rejoice. In the same manner God rejoices over a sinner, who was thought to be lost, is found". God's forgiving nature was illustrated with the parable of the prodigal son. A certain rich man had two sons. The younger one went to his father and asked for his share of the property. The father agreed and the son sold his share and moved to a distant city and enjoyed life with his friends. When he ran out of money, his friends left him. Meanwhile, there was a great famine. The young man found work in a pig farm. But what he got there was not enough to satisfy his hunger. Then it occurred to that his father's labourers ate better food than him. So he decided to go back to his father and ask for a labourer's job. His father spotted him from a distance, and went out and received him. He ordered fresh clothes for his son and asked his servants to kill the fattened calf and prepare a great feast to celebrate the return of his son. Meanwhile, the elder son, who was returning from the field, came back. He asked a servant what the fuss was about. He was told that there was great festivity to celebrate the return of his brother. He was upset at this and did not go into the house. The father went out to pacify him. But the son grumbled and complained that though he obeyed all the orders of the father, he never got such rewards. The father told him: "You are always with me and will inherit all my wealth. Your brother was lost, but has come back. He was dead for us, but now he is alive. Come and join the celebrations". There is great rejoicing in heaven, he said, when a sinner repents and returns to the fold.

Parables were also used to answer questions, especially of the tricky type. A certain young man went to Yeshua and asked;" Rabbi, what should I do to gain eternal life?"."What do the scriptures say?, asked Yeshua. The man replied: "the scriptures tell me to follow the Law. The Law tells us to love our neighbour. Please tell me who my neighbour is whom I should love?" Yeshua answered with a parable. A man was walking on the road from Jerusalem to Jericho. The winding road was notorious for mugging as the bends on the road allowed opportunities to make surprise attacks, and the bushes on either side gave ample cover for muggers to hide. The traveller was pounced upon by robbers, beaten up and robbed. He was left on the road to bleed to death. A priest, who chanced to pass by, walked away without even looking at the dying man. A Levite who was the next to pass by this road, looked at wounded man, but briskly walked on without offering any help. A Samaritan, who came next, stopped and dressed the wounds of the stricken man. He was then taken to the nearest inn, and left there to recuperate. He paid the inn keeper some money and offered to pay more, if necessary, on his return journey. Yeshua asked the questioner: "Which of the three passersby was a neighbour to the wounded traveller - the priest who is the representative of God, the Levite who is born to serve God or the Samaritan who is despised by the Jews?" The man answered that it was the Samaritan who was the best neighbour. Yeshua told him: "Now you have your answer. Your neighbour is the one who can help you in trouble, not the one who lives nearby or someone from your own community".

Yeshua believed in observing the Law in spirit, rather than in letter. This gave ample opportunity for his detractors to attack him for non-observance of the Law. Observance of the Sabbath is an example. The Law said that you should not work on Sabbath. As Yeshua and his disciples were walking through a cornfield, some disciples plucked ears of corn and chewed them. Soon accusations came that they were violating the Law. Similar charges were levelled when he healed the sick on the Sabbath day. Yeshua said: "The problem is with your understanding of work. If your lamb falls in a well on Sabbath day, will you not rescue it? If your father or mother falls ill on Sabbath, will you not minister to them? So you know there are exceptions and marginal cases. They do not violate the Law. Healing a sick person is not work for personal gain but it is a noble service. Therefore, healing is not prohibited by the Law".

The Pharisees and the Sadducees tried to trick him into making statements which could be taken against him. For example, they brought before him a woman caught in adultery. They asked him: "Rabbi, what shall we do with her?" They thought that whichever way Yeshua answered he would get caught. The Law clearly stated that a woman who committed adultery should be stoned to death. If Yeshua did not go along with the Law, he can be accused of going against it. On the other hand, if he endorsed stoning to death, his message of love and forgiveness would sound hollow. In the event, Yeshua said: "He that is without sin among you, let him cast the first stone". Nobody came forward to cast a stone. Yeshua looked at the bewildered woman and said: "Go and sin no more". On another occasion his detractors asked Yeshua whether it was right to pay tribute to the Roman Caesar. They thought that whether he said yes or no, he would get caught. The answer yes would mean that he was against the Jewish self respect. The answer no could be interpreted as treason against Caesar. But Yeshua took a different track. He said: "Give to Caesar what is Caesar's and to God what is God's". It would be too simplistic to consider Yeshua's answer as a clever dodging of the question. In fact, he was enunciating a new principle of separation of the State and Religion. The two should not interfere in each other's domain, unless it was for the violation of moral principles.

Yeshua generally referred to himself as Son of Man, clearly stressing his human origin. He never claimed any divine origin. Of course, he referred to God as his father, but all Jews claimed that they were children of God. He said: "The foxes have holes, the birds have nests, but the son of man has no place to rest his head". This was consistent with the fact that he never owned any property. He healed many people who were ill. However, he never claimed any supernatural powers. He attributed the healing to God the Father. He forbade those who were healed against publicising his role in the healing. Not that this admonition prevented them from attributing their cure to Yeshua and hailing his divinity. There were also many in the crowds that followed Yeshua because they liked his message. He reinterpreted the Law by making it more humane and bringing in an intellectual justification to the dry rules. By and large, the Jews hated the enforcement of the Law by the priestly class. Yeshua's reinterpretation of the Law made it come alive, and put the responsibility of its observance on the individual rather than on the priests. The rigidity of the rules and their verbatim, mechanical implementation was relaxed by allowing for exceptions based on overriding values and principles. For example, the strict observance of the Sabbath was moderated by compassion for those who were sick and suffering, as brought out in the parable of the sheep that had fallen into a well on Sabbath day, or by excluding the casual plucking of an ear of corn while walking through the corn field on Sabbath, from the rigid rules. This relaxation was also evident in the forgiveness given to the woman accused of adultery, whom the Pharisees wanted to be stoned to death.

One day Yeshua and his disciples were walking from Jerusalem to Galilee on the trunk road passing through Samaria. The day was hot, and by the time they reached Samaria, they were hungry and thirsty. Yeshua sat down by Jacob's well, while his disciples went to the nearby village to buy some food. As he sat there, he saw a Samaritan woman coming to the well with a pitcher in hand, obviously to draw water. He could not help recalling the story attributed to Buddha under similar circumstances. Buddha, weary with walk, came to a well and asked a *chandala* [low caste] woman for water to quench his thirst. The woman was surprised and, in fact, shocked, as is clear from her response. "Sir, you are obviously tired after long wanderings, and this must be the reason that you are forgetting the big gulf between us. You are obviously from a high caste and I am from a low caste. According to the customs of our society, you cannot drink water from my pitcher". However, Buddha insisted on drinking water from her pitcher and that is taken as an indication that he as well as Buddhism abhors the caste system.

Yeshua was brought back from his reverie to the present by the sound of water being drawn from the well. He got up from his seat, walked over to the woman and asked for some water. She pointed out that she was one of the Samaritans whom Jews despised. "Is it proper for you to ask me for water?" she asked. Yeshua replied: "I am thirsty and you have water. Is it right for you to refuse me water?" She relented and said: "You are obviously a Rabbi who is above caste considerations. I will gladly give you water". After Yeshua quenched his thirst, she explained her background. "We are not as lowly as the Jews think. We are their cousins." Yeshua frowned: "How come?" She had her answer: "It is true that when the Assyrian King Sennacherib conquered the Northern Kingdom, we were transplanted to the eastern end of the empire. Luckily, during our sojourn there, we learned many new things from the teachers of the East. We learned that we could control our minds, and even our bodies, through meditation. We learned to give up greed, lust, arrogance and anger, which are the root causes of unhappiness in our lives. This helped us to live without strife. Yeshua told her that he himself had learned these things in his studies in the East. "But tell me one thing", he said, "how did you come back?". "This happened because the Persian Kings were more civilised than their predecessors. "When Jews were allowed to return to Judea, we were also permitted to return. But the bulk of the deportees preferred to stay back, because the life there was good. However, a few of our forefathers decided to come back here and draw water from Jacob's well". She then asked permission to leave and bring her husband to meet the learned Rabbi. Yeshua asked mischievously: "After giving up the four controlling influences in your life, are you now controlled by your husband?" She answered seriously: "He is no evil influence: he is my companion and partner. Now let me go and bring him to meet you" So saying, she ran to the village and told her husband and neighbours about the learned Rabbi she met at the well. All of them ran back to meet Yeshua. They marvelled at his teachings and begged him to stay back. Yeshua said: "I have come on a mission to the Jews and that is my first priority. The Samaritans said: "Sir, you speak the language of the great teachers who guided us during our sojourn in the East and you are a man of peace. Please stay with us as we need a Rabbi like you. If you stay with us you are safe, as we are not like the Jews. If you speak against the priestly hierarchy of the Jews, they will not hesitate to finish you off". Yeshua said that he was prepared for any eventuality. One of the Samaritans had a question to Yeshua: "Rabbi, I have heard about your teachings. There appears to be some resemblance between your sermons and the teachings of Buddha". Yeshua replied: "That is not surprising, as I studied Buddhism in Taxila University". He assured the Samaritans that someday he may come back, but at this point of time his first priority was for the Jews.

Meanwhile the disciples came back with the food they bought in the village. After the meal, Yeshua and his disciples resumed their walk to Galilee. As they walked, the disciples wanted to know about Buddhism. Yeshua explained to them that Buddha was a great thinker and teacher who lived in India about six centuries earlier. Buddha attained enlightenment after sitting in meditation for forty nine days. He thus developed a deep insight into human condition. "Is it true that your messages have drawn upon Buddha's teachings?" they persisted. "Of course, it is true. We must acquire knowledge from whatever source that is available to us. In this case the source is a great thinker. "Please give us an example of how you used Buddha's teachings in yours", asked Peter. "That is easy", replied Yeshua. "You recall my parable of the sower to illustrate how the message is received. It is adapted from a simile given by Buddha. He gave the example of filling up a vessel with milk. First there has to be an opening to pour milk through. The quantity of milk that reaches the vessel depends on the size of the opening. If the vessel is leaky, it will not get filled, as part of the milk will flow out. If the vessel is contaminated with bitter or poisonous material, the whole of the milk inside will be spoilt. Now compare it with the parable. The seeds in the parable replace the milk. The milk that is spilled outside on account of the small opening of the vessel represent the seeds which fall on the wayside or on stony ground. They are both lost. The milk that leaks out is parallel to the message that is heard, but not understood. The contamination in the vessel has its parallel in the shoots which are smothered by thorns. Buddha chose to talk about milk because he lived in a pastoral country. Here we are in fields of grain and hence a parable built around sowing is more appropriate. This is an example of how the message is communicated to the people, using analogies drawn from their day-to-day experience" "Are you saying that you prefer Buddhism to the faith of our fathers?" they asked. "No, that is not what i am saying", replied Yeshua. "I am trying to integrate the best ideas we can get from anywhere into our religion. Do remember that we have remained stagnant from the time of Moses. We must bring in new ideas and new knowledge where ever we can get them and thus enrich our religion. Not doing that is nothing short of arrogance."

Thomas asked: "Rabbi, You mentioned once about another great religion of the East. I forget what it was". "You must be referring to Hinduism. It is one of the oldest religions, which prevailed in that part of the world even before Buddhism. In fact, Buddha was born a Hindu." Thomas added: "I was wondering whether you benefitted from the teachings of this religion", Yeshua: "Hindu religion has plenty of scriptures, some dating back to ancient times. It is all composed in Sanskrit. I had to learn that language in order to understand their scriptures. Their oldest scriptures are known as Vedas. The oldest of these four Vedas is called Rig Veda, which consists of oblations to gods like *Indra* [lord of the sky and war], *Agni* [god of fire] and *Varuna* [god of water or sea]. Then they have their epics – Ramayana and Mahabharata. To answer your question whether I had benefitted from studying these scriptures, let me tell you that one always benefits from new knowledge. For example, the epic Ramayana is about a righteous King Rama, who ruled with justice and fair play. His reign is the Hindu equivalent of the Kingdom of God. The other epic, Mahabharata, contains the central theology of Hinduism in the form of Bhagawat Gita. In this, Krishna, God incarnate, admonishes Arjuna, his friend and warrior, to do his duty regardless of consequences. He also talks about establishing a righteous order. He points out the evil effects of *kama* [lust], *krodha* [anger], *lobha* [greed] and *mada* [arrogance] in human life. All religions have their good points. Wise people accept the good and reject the rest. Unfortunately, most people get carried away by mythology and ignore the theology."

As they continued their walk, John asked him: "Rabbi, don't you think that the Samaritan woman was surprisingly knowledgeable and articulate?" "You are right, John", replied Yeshua. "God created man and woman with the same level of intelligence. Man is physically stronger, and for this reason he controls the woman. This has happened throughout history. When you read our scriptures, it is seen that women have been treated as non-entities. For example, the number of men who left Egypt in exodus is mentioned, but the number of women is not given. They are clubbed together with children and cattle without mentioning their number. It is as though the loss of a few did not matter. The same is the case with the march back from Babylonian sojourn. In our society, women are not found in any leadership position. Polygamy was widely prevalent, permitting a man to have several wives, which means equality was unheard of. Solomon had seven hundred wives and three hundred concubines, a sure indication that women were treated like commodity. I am glad that our Samaritan friends are treating their women with respect. This is where we can learn some lessons from other societies. What a difference it would make if women, who are numerically equal to men, are allowed to make their contributions to society!" John recalled that Yeshua was treating his women followers with courtesy and respect. Women like Mary Magdalene worked closely with him in his healing mission, but there was not even a hint of any gender based involvement between them. Yet he listened to them, answered their questions and gave instructions where necessary. Even his attitude to his family [father, mother and brothers] was exemplary. He treated them with courtesy and affection, but never allowed them to interfere with his mission. John remembered the occasion when his mother Salome came to visit Yeshua and requested a special favour from him. She wanted her sons, James and John, to sit on his right and his left when he established his Kingdom. Yeshua scolded them and said: "It is not known to me what responsibility I will have in the Kingdom of God, nor do I know who will sit next to me. These are in the hands of God, our Father".

One day Nicodemos came to meet Yeshua with a message from the High Priest. He said that the Sanhedrin, in a recent meeting, discussed Yeshua's mission and his popularity. It was decided that a delegation should hold a meeting with Yeshua, and work out a compromise so that a confrontation can be avoided. Nicodemos's mission was to fix a meeting. Yeshua said that he was willing to meet such a delegation and suggested the place and time of the meeting. Accordingly a twelve member committee of the Sanhedrin led by Chief Priest Obadiah and comprising Sadducees, Pharisees and Rabbis met Yeshua. They proposed that Yeshua should stop preaching against the Law of Moses and denigrating the priests. In return they were willing accept

Yeshua as a Rabbi, thus throwing open all the synagogues and the Temple of Jerusalem for Yeshua to preach. The Sanhedrin was also willing to support him financially. Yeshua said: "I have repeatedly stated that I have come to fulfil the Law and not to disrupt it." "But you have spoken against the Law on divorces and the Law on punishment for sins like adultery, as well as tit-for-tat response for wrong doings like physical attack". Yeshua replied: "You must remember that Moses gave the Law at a time when women were treated as lowly creatures,. Also, please note that adultery cannot be committed by one person alone. Both parties to the crime must be punished equally. As the law does not provide for this, we should go to the root cause of the problem which is lust. That is what should be eschewed. We must recognise that the Law of Moses was a great improvement over prevailing norms, but was not perfect. If you strictly enforce 'an eye for an eye and a tooth for a tooth' Law, we will end up with blind and toothless men everywhere. The cycle can be broken only with forgiveness and compassion". "But you have no authority to change the Law that YHWH gave us through Moses", countered the delegation. Yeshua responded: "My mission is to fulfil the Law by making it conform to current norms which are practised in more advanced societies. Obscurantist people will be left behind in the dust heaps of history". The Chief Priest noted that there was no meeting ground on this issue, and moved on to the second issue of denigration of the priests. Yeshua responded by saying; "I have not denigrated all priests. I have criticised some priests who live in the past. I have also pointed out the hypocrisy of some Pharisees who make a public display of their fasting and praying. Such behaviour is inconsistent with true prayer and fasting". The chief priest declared that their effort for a harmonious relationship had failed and they would report to the Sanhedrin.

Forgiveness was central to his message. Peter asked him:"Rabbi, How many times should I forgive my brother - will seven times do?" Yeshua answered: "That is not enough; I would say seventy times seven. It is your attitude to others that matters. It is necessary to view others with compassion". He illustrated it with a parable. A certain King decided to settle his accounts with his employees. He called one of them who owed him 10,000 Talents. As the man could not pay it off, the King decided to sell him, his wife, children and all his belongings *to* recover the money. The man fell at the King's feet and begged for mercy. The King took pity on the hapless debtor and forgave the entire debt. As the man went out he saw a colleague who owed him 100 denirii. Forgetting that his debt was greater by 60000 times what his colleague owed him, he caught his debtor by the neck and threatened to put him in jail, ignoring his own plea for mercy. Some of those who witnessed this reported it to the King, who ordered that this person should be given to the torturers till he paid his debt. He said "You were forgiven 10,0000 talents, but you cannot reschedule a 100 denirii of debt". Similarly our Father in heaven will not forgive our sins, if we are intolerant to even minor errors of our neighbours. We must learn to forgive others as God, our father forgives us.

After he gave his messages to large crowds in the towns around the Sea of Galilee, Yeshua decided to revisit the places on the left bank of River Jordan, where he concentrated in the initial days of his mission, This also gave him some time for introspection. He was on his mission for over three years. In the process he developed a big following. Not only did crowds follow him wherever he went, his sermons he were well attended. His audience always wanted more of his teaching. 'What next?' was the question which was uppermost in his mind. So Yeshua retreated into the wilderness for a session of meditation. He weighed the pros and cons of all possibilities in front of him. He had reached the peak of his popularity as a Rabbi and a preacher. 'How long should this be continued? What is the point?' he thought for himself. On the other hand, he asked himself: 'What was he really after?". He was not after political power. Nor did he aspire to be the High Priest or even a Chief Priest. He was against all forms of violence and that was what he taught. Even on practical terms, a violent uprising would be against the political authority, which was the Roman Government. They were far too powerful militarily to be overthrown. His mission was to liberate the Jews from the strangle hold of the priestly hierarchy. An onslaught on the Sanhedrin, especially the High Priest and Pharisees would be necessary to achieve his goal. This could be achieved only by winning over the large crowd that gathers in the Temple of Jerusalem during the festival of Passover. He would be safe so long as he was surrounded by a crowd of followers. The best time for this action was only a few days ahead, when all Jews would gather in Jerusalem. Yeshua asked his disciples to get ready for a trip to Jerusalem.

As they trudged along the uneven road on the left bank of River Jordan that led to Jerusalem, he realised that his plans could go awry. If the agents of the High Priest caught him, they would try to eliminate him. After all he had been attacking the very foundations of their power. As he thought of this possibility and its consequences, his face became dark with foreboding. His disciples noted this and questioned him about it. He told them: "It is important that we should be prepared for all eventualities. It is quite possible that I may get killed in Jerusalem. I want you people to continue with the mission even if I am eliminated", he told them. The disciples were frightened at what their Master had said. They looked at each other in bewilderment. As they walked along, they came to a tall hill. Yeshua asked his disciples to remain at the bottom, but motioned to three of them - Peter, James and his brother John - to accompany him up the hill. As they reached near the top, he asked his three associates to stay back and pray, while he went to the mountain top to commune with God the Father. He walked to the top of the hill and sat in his favourite lotus position. The disciples noticed that he was talking to someone. Then a cloud appeared and surrounded Yeshua making him invisible to the trio. As they were wondering what happened, there was a lightning and the cloud disappeared from the scene. They saw Yeshua walking downhill towards them. The continuing lightning put a halo over his head and his face was bright and shining in the flashing light. As he approached closer, Peter asked: "Whom were you speaking to? When you went up your face looked dark and troubled. But now your face shines like the son". Yeshua replied: "I was speaking to my Father in heaven. When I went up I was anxious about my future course of action. But now my mind is made up and I am at peace with myself. Now let us go to Jerusalem".

CHAPTER 9

From Hosannas to Crucifixion

As Yeshua's party approached Jerusalem, he decided to camp at Bethany. This place was close to Jerusalem, where he was planning his final showdown with the ecclesiastical authorities, but it was also safe as it was an Essene stronghold. Not only did Yeshua feel safe here, but he was also sure of infrastructural support for his mission. As the first day of the Passover week arrived after the Sabbath, he called two of his disciples and asked them to proceed to the town. "As soon as you enter the town, you will find an ass and a colt tied to their stakes. Untie the colt and bring it here. If anyone asks, you tell him that your Master has need for it". The disciples did as they were told. Meanwhile, the Essene leaders came and assured Yeshua that all arrangements for his triumphant entry into the city were in place. The disciples put their cloaks on the colt for Yeshua to sit and ride. As he reached the high road to Jerusalem, a large crowd greeted him. Some went ahead of him, while others came behind. All of them were shouting: *Hosanna to the Son of David, the Messiah who has come to redeem Israel.* As they moved towards the city more people joined the procession. The large number of pilgrims, who had already arrived in the city, came out to see the procession. They wanted to know what was happening. The accompanying crowd told them: "This is Yeshua, the Messiah from Nazareth". The whole city was agog with the news of the Messiah's arrival.

With the crowd in tow, Yeshua entered the temple. In the courtyard itself, he saw flourishing commercial establishments like those selling animals and birds for sacrificial offerings. While the wealthy pilgrims sacrificed a goat, the poor would offer a pigeon or a sparrow. There were also desks of money changers as well as those of collectors of temple tax. He threw out the dealers in animals and birds and over turned the tables of money changers, saying: "Haven't you heard it said that this is a house of God. But you are making it a den of thieves". The large crowd that witnessed this cleansing operation, cheered Yeshua. He used the opportunity to preach to them about the Kingdom of God, which would soon get established. As usual he spoke in parables. He likened the Kingdom of God to a vineyard, whose owner went about recruiting labourers to work on the vines. He went to the market place in the morning and hired whoever was available, at an agreed rate. He went again at noon and hired some more workers. He made another trip in the afternoon and picked up some more labourers. Finally he made a last trip a little before closing time. This group worked only for an hour before wages were distributed. The owner of the vineyard paid everybody the same wage. Those who came in early complained that they should have received more than the latecomers. But the owner was firm, explaining that he paid everybody the agreed wages. In spite of the apparent unfairness when viewed from the angle of correlation between hours of work and wages, it is perfectly logical from the point of view of the Kingdom of God. The reward is admission to the Kingdom. Once you are admitted, you enjoy the same benefits as those who were already inside.

When it was evening Yeshua went back his temporary lodging in Bethany where he felt secure. Next day also he went to the Temple and spoke to the crowds assembled there. His theme continued to be the Kingdom of God and he spoke in parables. For example, he told the parable of the Big Feast. A certain king organised a great feast and invited all the dignitaries of the land. But none of them came for the feast. So he sent his messengers to remind them of the invitation. They did not care even to respond. Then the king asked his assistants to go to the thoroughfares and bring in whomsoever they saw. This had to be done a couple of times before the dining hall was full. The King went around greeting his guests and found a man who was not wearing the appropriate dress. He was thrown out. Thus the dignitaries missed out on the feast, but the ordinary people got in provided they were prepared. Yeshua concluded by saying that when the Kingdom of God is established, those who were ahead in society may become the last, and those who were lowly may enter first. The Pharisees realised that he was speaking about them, but could only seethe within, as the crowd was clearly on Yeshua's side. He also healed many sick people who were brought to him.

Two days before the Feast of the Passover, his disciples asked Yeshua where they should prepare the Passover meal. He told them to go to the town and look for a man carrying a pitcher of water. They realised that it was easy to spot; as a man carrying a pitcher of water was an unusual sight. Normally, it was the job of womenfolk to go to the common well and fetch water. If they saw a man drawing water it was an Essene house where only celibates lived. And sure enough, they saw a man carrying a pitcher of water and followed him to his house. They told the head of the household that they were sent by their Rabbi who wanted to know where he could celebrate the Passover with his disciples. Without any hesitation, he showed them an upper room which was furnished for their Passover meal. The disciples arranged the supper on Passover day in the upper room as directed by the Master. When they sat around the table, Yeshua took the bread in his hand, blessed it and gave it to them, saying: *take and eat it in memory of the Passover.* Similarly he lifted the wine in his hand, blessed it and asked them to drink it in memory of the original Passover. He added: *even if I am not with you next year, do these in remembrance of me.* Simon Peter protested and said: "Rabbi, why are you saying such things? You must be always with us". "It is not given to you or me to know what lies ahead. But I realise that the authorities of the Temple are looking for me with the idea of eliminating me. Their last chance is tonight, because they dare not arrest me during the day time when I am in the midst of people. By eventide tomorrow, the Sabbath starts and before it ends I would leave Jerusalem", replied Yeshua. Peter continued: "They do not know where you are going to be tonight. So you are safe". "There is one possibility that you have ignored. Peter. One of you can betray me and inform the High Priest where I am", replied Yeshua. "Who will do such a heinous act? Not me", said several disciples in unison. "We will soon find out who will stand by me and who will deny ever knowing me". Peter protested and said: "Whatever happens, I will not deny you". Yeshua told him: "When the time comes you will deny me, not once but three times. Meanwhile, I am going to the Mount of Olives for meditation. If you like, you can accompany me".

All the disciples followed Yeshua to the Mount of Olives. He asked them to wait there in the Garden of Gethsamane and pray, while he moved forward to a point a stone's throw away and communed with the Father in Heaven. He prayed: "Father, if possible let this cup pass from me. Yet it is not my will, but Your Will that will be done". After a while he returned to find the disciples heavy with sleep. He told them: "All I asked of you was that you pray for yourselves to keep out of temptation, but you could not even keep awake. But now you can sleep all you want, as my hour has come". Even as he spoke these words, Judas Iscariot was approaching them, leading a group of armed guards sent by the High Priest. Judas walked up to Yeshua, greeted him and kissed him on the cheek. This was the sign for the guards to arrest Yeshua. There was some resistance from the rest of the disciples, like one of them taking out a sword. But Yeshua discouraged any violence. Anyway, it was too little in front of the armed might of the palace guards. Once Yeshua was taken by the guards, the disciples fled from the scene. Only Peter followed at a distance.

Yeshua was taken to the palace of the High Priest, where all the dignitaries had gathered to conduct a trial. In addition to the Hugh Priest, there were the chief priests and some important functionaries of the Sanhedrin, sitting in their designated seats on the podium. Only a partisan crowd was permitted into the quadrangle. Several false witnesses were brought to testify against Yeshua, but none could give a reasonable charge. Finally they found two people who testified that Yeshua claimed to be Son of God. The High Priest claimed that this was blasphemy. He asked; 'Are you really son of God?' Yeshua answered: "You said it, not me". At this the High Priest said, pretending not to have heard the second part: "This is blasphemy. The punishment is death". Some members of the Sanhedrin pointed out that though the Law prescribed death penalty, it can be awarded only by the Roman Governor. But the Governor could be approached only during the day. So the period until the Governor sits in his seat of judgement was used to physically torture Yeshua. He was beaten with thongs, spat upon and hit in the face with hands. The guards clearly relished doing it. A crown of thorns was placed on his head and forced down with the result that blood trickled down on his beard. He was mocked as the King of Israel. All this while, Peter was standing or sitting crouched with a crest fallen face. A maid first saw him and asked him whether he was with Yeshua. He denied it and moved away. A second maid then confronted him, but Peter denied any knowledge of the prisoner. When it happened a third time, Peter remembered the words of his Rabbi and went out and wept bitterly.

In the morning they bound him and marched him to the court of Pontius Pilate, the Governor of Judea. Judas Iscariot saw this and was overcome by remorse for what he had done. He did not intend that this should happen to the Master whom he followed for three years. He genuinely believed that Yeshua was the Son of God who would usher in the Kingdom of God. All he wanted was to hasten the establishment of that Kingdom, in which he expected to get a high position. He calculated that when the armed guards arrived, God would send his angels to ensure the victory of his son and that would mark the beginning of the new Kingdom. He condemned himself for his selfish miscalculation and went to return the thirty pieces of silver that he got as reward for his betrayal. The High Priest's party refused to take it back. So he threw it to them and went and hanged himself. The crowd that followed Yeshua earlier in the day did not have any clue about his whereabouts. Anyway, they had retired for the night. The disciples themselves were scattered and did not know what to do.

The High Priest's party presented Yeshua before the Roman Governor with a plea to crucify him for blasphemy. But according to Roman Laws there was no provision for death penalty for blasphemy. So without going into the merits of the case, Pontius Pilate offered to release Yeshua following the custom of releasing a prisoner at the time of the Passover Feast. Since this was to be done on the basis of a popular request, Pilate asked those assembled in the courtyard whether he could release Yeshua. However, the highly partisan crowd rejected this offer, and wanted a robber named Barabbas to be released. Meanwhile, Pilate found out that Yeshua was a Galilean, and referred the case to Herod Antipas, the ruler of Galilee who happened to be in Jerusalem. Antipas, who had already heard about Yeshua did not wish to get involved. So he sent Yeshua back to Pilate on the ground that though the prisoner was born in Galilee, the alleged crime was committed in Jerusalem. So Pilate had to make up his mind. He asked the petitioners to present the case and call witnesses. But there was nothing in the presentations to show that Yeshua was guilty of treason which was the only ground on which death penalty could be awarded. Meanwhile Pilate got some private requests from some members of the Sanhedrin that no harsh punishment should be handed down. On the other hand, his instruction from Caesar was that an armed revolt should be avoided, as it was difficult send an army unit to quell the rebellion. It was possible, he thought, that the Jewish hierarchy can use this occasion to promote a rebellion. As a bureaucrat he washed his hands off ceremonially and declared that he did not want any part in shedding the blood of this innocent man.

The chief priests went back and requested Pilate to issue formal orders for crucifixion. They wanted this process to be expedited because it was already preparation day before Sabbath, and hence the entire process including the burial of the body had to be completed before sunset. Pilate thought it best to agree, as he did not want to antagonise the priestly hierarchy. He ordered a detachment of troops under a Centurion to supervise the crucifixion. Meanwhile, the prisoner was under the control of the High Priest's militia. They mocked him, put the crown of thorn back on his head and scourged him. This went on until the Roman troops took charge. They went about their task strictly as per rules. The place of crucifixion was a hilltop called Calvary. As was the practice, the condemned man was made to carry the wooden cross. Seeing him falter, the Centurion asked Simon of Cyrene to carry it, while the soldiers egged him on with scourges in hand. The motley crowd that followed this procession was mostly partisans of the High Priest. Some women who were close to Yeshua, including his mother Miriam and Mary Magdalene, followed in the rear, weeping profusely. The soldiers ensured that nobody came near Yeshua. At the hilltop, Yeshua was nailed to the cross at his hands and feet. As an added precaution his hands and feet were tied to the beams. A board was fixed on top of the cross with the inscription which read: YESHUA of NAZARETH KING OF JEWS in three languages. The representatives of the High Priest objected to this, but the centurion overruled them. It was warm and sunny when the cross was raised and secured in vertical position. Two robbers were also crucified on either side of Yeshua. The whole operation was over by the time the first quarter of the day was over.

The crowd of onlookers included Jewish partisans who mocked Yeshua with phrases like: 'Physician, heal thyself', but also his crestfallen followers. Yeshua saw his mother in the crowd, and called his youngest disciple John and asked him to take care of her. Even the robbers on either side differed from each other. One mocked Yeshua but the other said: "We are paying for our sins. But what sin has this innocent man done?" Yeshua continued to groan from pain. When he called his father in heaven, some people thought that he was calling Prophet Elijah. As the sun reached its peak position in the sky, it became hot and Yeshua shouted that he was thirsty. 'I have just the right drink for you', thought the centurion. Indeed he had a concoction which, he said, was a mixture of wine and vinegar. He fed it to Yeshua through a reed dipping into his flask. Though he didn't like the taste, the prisoner drank most of it as he was very thirsty. As the day moved on to the afternoon, it became quite cloudy, which was not unusual for this region. There was a breeze blowing across Calvary which appeared to have put Yeshua to sleep. As the third quarter of the day ended Yeshua was hanging on the cross with his head drooping to one side. His posture gave the impression that he was dead. "Let us confirm that he is dead", said the centurion. He poked the sharp end of his spear to the side of the hanging body. "Just as I thought", said the centurion, "It is blood mixed with water. Proof enough that he is dead". Since centurion was the authority to declare whether the crucified man was dead or alive; his statement was the final word. The soldiers helped to bring down Yeshua's body. It was put on a trolley which could be rolled over to the tomb.

Meanwhile Yosef of Arimathea went to Pontius Pilate and got permission to bury Yeshua in a nearby tomb. The Jewish hierarchy was not very happy about it, but they could not challenge the Governor's decision. They petitioned the. Governor to post guards at the tomb so that Yeshua's followers could not steal the body, and then claim that he rose from the dead. Governor Pilate told them: "You have a good militia. Why don't you mount the guard yourselves?" They consulted among themselves and decided to post guards after Sabbath.

CHAPTER 10

Escape from the Gallows

Unknown to Yeshua, several efforts were being made to save him from the maneuverings of the High Priests. Yosef of Arimathea met Pontius Pilate on Passover night itself and got an assurance from him that he would offer to release Yeshua as the traditional gesture at the time of the Passover. However, this did not work out. Yeshua's supporters were not present in the courtyard where Pilate sat in the seat of judgment. The crowd that followed Yeshua during the previous day had all retired for the night, and they had no clue about his whereabouts. The High Priest's guards allowed only their hand-picked partisans into the courtyard. Thus when Pilate offered to release Yeshua, the crowd shouted "Barabbas", the robber, as their choice for pardon on the occasion of the Passover. Pilate felt helpless, as his instructions from Caesar were not to antagonize the Jews. This was because Rome was not in a position to spare more troops in the eventuality of a revolt. So Pilate washed his hands off and declared that he had no share in the blood of this righteous man. However, his action meant that he tacitly acquiesced to crucifixion, in order to save his skin, caught as he was between the Jewish hierarchy and the authorities in Rome. Later that morning, Yosef along with Nicodemus, another member of the Sanhedrin, met Pilate again. The purpose was to find a way for saving Yeshua. They pointed out that the huge crowds that followed Yeshua would curse Pilate forever. Moreover, they offered a substantial sum of money to Pilate for his help. Pilate said that the best he could do at this stage was to nominate a friendly Centurion to take charge of the squad that would supervise the crucifixion. Accordingly, Longinus was assigned the task, with the added instruction to save Yeshua's life, if possible. Pilate knew that Longinus was an admirer of Yeshua and had attended some his sermons. Longinus made sure that the guards of the High Priest did not harm the prisoner in anyway. Though some of them insisted that the condemned man should carry the cross, Longinus asked Simon of Cyrene to carry it, thus saving Yeshua the burden. When they reached Calvary, the appointed hill top for crucifixion, he and his armed soldiers made sure that nobody came near the cross. When Yeshua was nailed to the cross, he took care that only a minimum number of nails was used and that they did not pierce the bones. Further Yeshua's hands and feet were tied to the beams to minimize pain from the hanging effect at the nails. He made sign boards in three languages which read: "Yeshua, King of Jews" and fixed them on top of the cross, overruling the objections of the priests. The two robbers who were hanged on either side of Yeshua got none of these privileges. After a few hours on the cross, when Yeshua said he was thirsty, Longinus was ready with a concoction that he had prepared by spiking wine with a narcotic. It was offered to Yeshua to drink through a reed. Though he did not like the taste, Yeshua drank it. He said loudly: "My God, My God", and lost consciousness. It was now the job of the centurion to determine whether the crucified man was dead or alive. Longinus poked the body of Yeshua with his spear and said that the fluid which came out was blood mixed with water, which meant that the man on the cross was dead. After pronouncing Yeshua dead, he declared that there was no need to break his legs. This is in contrast to the treatment meted out to the two robbers who were crucified alongside Yeshua. Since they were not dead before sunset, their legs were broken before they were lowered from the cross. In the case of Yeshua, the Centurion helped Yosef of Arimathea and Nicodemos to lower the body on to a cart, which served as a hearse, for taking it to the tomb. The centurion also used his soldiers to prevent anybody from following the body to the tomb. By sunset it was Sabbath and no Jew would walk to the tomb. It was a newly made sepulcher hewn out of the side of a rock, located in a garden, which was recently purchased by Yosef of Arimathea. Its proximity to Calvary suggested that Yosef had this eventuality in mind when he made it. The Jewish leaders petitioned the Roman administration to secure the tomb with guards so that the disciples did not take away the body and claim that their master had risen from the dead, but Pontius Pilate took the view that it was an internal matter of the Jews. The Jewish hierarchy decided that no action was immediately necessary as Sabbath was beginning soon. The posting of a guard at the tomb was postponed until after Sabbath.

The tomb was of the type that wealthy Jews made for their family, with provision for the interment of several bodies. It was cut into the side of a small hillock of soft stone. The entry was through a square opening through which a person could enter only by bending down. This opening could be closed or opened by rolling a circular stone block into position. The opening was obviously sized to match with the stone cover which required four or five able bodied men to move into place through a channel cut on the ground. Entry through the door led to a cavern, its floor one step below the ground level. On the two sides of the cavern, there were raised platforms.

The walls of the platforms were carved out to form shelves. Dead bodies wrapped up in linen, or sarcophagi, could be pushed into these shelves. On the fourth side of the cavern, a stone slab was located as a bench on which a dead body could be prepared for burial. Yeshua's body was placed on the stone slab.

The three Essene volunteers, who were assigned the task of attending to Yeshua, arrived at the sepulcher after sunset and took charge of the body. Nicodemus had come prepared with a good quantity of *Aloe Vera* and other herbs which could be used to heal wounds. Yosef had sent a message to Mary Magdalene to bring her medicine chest to the sepulcher, and this she did dutifully. She came full of anxiety for the Rabbi, but Yosef simply told her that they were trying to save him, and they may have some news by Sunday morning. Meanwhile, she was sworn to secrecy, and advised to keep out of the way of High Priest's guards. The Essenes crushed the Aloe Vera to extract its juice and mixed it with some ointments found in the medicine chest and started professionally to dress all the wounds on the body. These wounds were at places on hands and feet where nails went through, on the head where thorns pierced through the skin when a crown of thorns was cruelly pressed down, on the back where he was whipped in the High Priest's courtyard and on the torso where a lance cut the skin. Their aim, they explained, was to complete the dressing before Yeshua regained consciousness. Meanwhile, Yosef rummaged through the medicine chest and found a packet labeled as *sanjivani*. When he opened the packet, he found a note in Aramaic. It said that sanjivani was the last resort for those who have sustained serious wounds in fighting, and were suffering from high fever. One packet of powder should be dissolved in a glass of water and given to the patient. Only if the fever did not subside in six hours after the first dose, should a second dose be administered. Under no circumstances should more than two doses be given to one patient. The medicine was so strong that only a healthy person can tolerate even two doses. A third dose was likely to end in the patient's death.

As the evening progressed, the Essenes reported that Yeshua had developed high fever. They placed wet clothes on the patient's forehead and chest to control the fever, but the clothes had to be frequently wetted to keep them moist. By midnight Yeshua started grunting and groaning, suggesting that he was in great pain. At this point Yosef decided to give a dose of sanjivani. The patient continued to groan with eyes closed, and the fever refused to come down. When the fever continued to rage even at dawn, Yosef decided to give the second dose. Nicodemus advised caution. He argued that Yeshua's body was already quite weak, as he had to suffer torture all through the previous night and this was followed by crucifixion during the day. But Yosef did not agree. He said: "if we give the second dose, we are at least trying to save his life. Otherwise, the fever will claim his life". The Essene novices chipped in to say that the fever was too high and in that condition the patient was unlikely to survive more than a few hours. Yosef went ahead and administered the second dose. The Essenes continued their ministrations. Just before noon on the Sabbath day, the patient started sweating profusely. The attendants kept wiping out the sweat. Slowly the fever started to subside. Twenty four hours after the centurion pronounced him dead on the cross, Yeshua opened his eyes and asked for water, which was given. Then he dozed off to sleep. At sunset, a new team of Essenes replaced the tired threesome that took care of the patient so far. They persuaded Yosef and Nicodemos to go home, as Yeshua was clearly improving. Further, they had to conserve their strength to face the challenges of the next day, when the High Priest's men would come to find out where the crucified man's body had gone. This time the team was headed by a senior leader of the Essenes named Daniel. He pointed out to Yosef the challenges that lay ahead. He said: "Please remember that Yeshua was pronounced dead by the centurion who represented Roman authorities. If Yeshua falls into the hands of the Jewish authorities, they may kill him and produce the body claiming that the disciples stole it. Today being Sabbath, they may not be active. But tomorrow morning they will start their search. Our plan is to take

Yeshua to a secret retreat on the mountain for recuperation. It is importamt that we should take him away before dawn tomorrow. Our immediate concern is to make sure that he is able travel to our destination by that time. So please leave him alone and go and get some rest. Before you leave, there is one small thing you have to do. Yeshua's clothes were taken away by the soldiers at the cross. So we have a problem of how to clothe him. We had not anticipated this situation. I looked around this place a little while ago. There is a garden kiosk outside which is locked. I would like to look in there for some clothes". So they went out and Yosef opened the kiosk, using a key from his key bunch. The only dress they could find was a gardener's overall and cap. 'I suppose we have to make do with this', Daniel said.

Before it was dawn, they managed to get Yeshua on his feet and dressed him in the gardener's outfit. They took him outside to wait for the horse drawn cart that was on the way. They briefly went inside to pick up their gear. It was at this time, when it was still dark, that Mary Magdalene arrived on the scene and mistook the white-clad Essenes for angels. She went outside and saw Yeshua in the gardener's uniform, but could not recognize him because his long hair and flowing beard were cut before crucifixion. Seeing Mary's anxiety and grief, Yeshua said: "Mary!" Mary recognized the voice and went close to him, exclaiming: 'Rabboni!' Seeing her approach, Yeshua told her not to come any closer, but go and inform the others that he was alive. Soon after she left, the Essenes came out and helped Yeshua onto the horse cart which had just arrived. They drove off to the secure house on the hill. When the other disciples came, they saw only the empty tomb, with strips of linen lying on the floor. It is only natural that they thought that their master had risen from the dead.

Under the diligent ministration of the Essenes, Yoshua rapidly recovered. He was first allowed to walk around the retreat. Then he was permitted to take longer walks during the twilight period before dawn or after sunset. The High Priest and his guards looked for him, or the dead body, high and low, but could not find any clue. They arranged surveillance of the disciples with no result. In one of the twilight walks, Yeshua saw two of his people on the road to Emmaus. Yeshua joined them and found that they were talking about the report that their master had risen from the dead. They did not recognize him because he was without his long beard as well as locks of hair which were cut off before crucifixion. The two men decided to stop for supper at an inn, and invited Yeshua to join them. When he took the bread in his hands, gave thanks and broke it, they recognized him. They then decided to return immediately to Jerusalem to tell the news to their friends. Meanwhile, Yeshua slipped out and walked back with the waiting Essenes. Now Yeshua told Daniel that he was keen to meet the disciples and assure them that he was alive. Andrew was summoned to plan a visit at night without arousing suspicion, as Yeshua's life was still in danger, with the Jewish militia looking for him or his dead body. Andrew arranged the meeting in an upper room where the disciples were meeting. Escorted by Essene guards, Yeshua went to Jerusalem after sunset, and entered the dimly lit upper room through a back door, which was opened by Andrew. Suddenly Yeshua was standing in the midst of the disciples. When he greeted them with the words: "Peace be with you", they recognized him. He assured them that he was alive and disappeared the way he came. They thought that it was Yeshua who had risen from the dead who was standing in front of them. After all, they witnessed his death on the cross. Thomas was not present when Yeshua presented himself to the disciples. Next day, when the event was explained to him, he refused to believe it, saying that until he had himself seen the master and examined the scars of his wounds, he would not believe the story. So Yeshua made another visit, this time after Andrew ensured the presence of Thomas. Thomas put his fingers into the scars in the hand and side of the master, and was satisfied. Yeshua again disappeared into the darkness.

Daniel and his colleagues decided that it was not safe for Yeshua to move about even after dark, because they got reliable information that the Jewish authorities had intensified their search, after rumours started spreading that Yeshua had risen from the dead. Nicodemus confirmed this information through his sources in the Sanhedrin. After some discussion, it was decided that Yeshua should move to Edessa. This was based on the fact that Edessa was an independent city state, where neither the Jews nor the Romans had much influence. Moreover, the ruler of Edessa had earlier sent a request to Yeshua to visit Edessa and heal some members of the royal family. When Yeshua was told about the plan, he agreed, but with one modification. He wanted a halt at Galilee to meet his disciples one last time. As Galilee was on the way to Edessa, Daniel readily agreed. Andrew was given the responsibility of informing the disciples. A few days later, Yeshua started his journey north by horse cart. Daniel and two Essene novices escorted him. They traveled mostly by night to avoid encounter with High Priest's militia. At Galilee they stayed in an Essene retreat in the hills. Well before dawn the next day, Yeshua walked over to the lake shore, where he expected to find his disciples fishing. Indeed Peter along with Thomas, and James and John (sons of Zebedee), Nathaniel of Cana and two others were already in their fishing boats. They were fishing all night, but caught nothing. Then they saw Yeshua coming towards them, wading through the shallow waters. "Have you caught anything?" he asked. "No", shouted Peter. "Then cast your net on the right side of the boat", suggested Yeshua. "We were doing that all night, but caught nothing", protested Peter. "I noticed that you had cast your net on the left side. Therefore, I asked you to cast your nets on the right side", explained Yeshua. They did so and caught their nets full of fish. When they dragged their catch to the shore, they saw Yeshua sitting there with a fire burning to broil the fish. There was also some bread. Yeshua asked them to bring some fish they have caught. When it was ready, he raised the bread in his hand, gave thanks and gave it to them to eat with the fish. Then he enjoined them to continue the movement to establish the Kingdom of God on earth. He told them that he would be gone for quite a while and did not know when he would return. But when he did, he would like to see the Kingdom established. He enjoined them to spread his message to all people. Then he was gone.

Yeshua went back to the lodge and found Daniel and his two associates ready for travel. The journey was uneventful. Daniel knew what route to take and when, so that they would not run into the search party. They stopped only once for rest, and that was in an inn under the control of the Essenes. Once they crossed over to Edessaa, they heaved a sigh of relief. Edessa was a city state which managed to keep out of the power struggle between two big countries. It was strategically located on the silk route and profited from the long distance trade stretching from China in the east and to Rome in the west. They had the Roman Empire on the west and the Parthian Empire on the east. Yeshua and party were received by King Akbar V himself. They were lodged in the royal guest house located next to the palace. Daniel was pleased with this arrangement because even spies sent by the Jewish hierarchy would find it difficult to cross the security guards of the palace. Yeshua could, meanwhile, walk around the palace ground, especially the well tended palace gardens. King Akbar had heard about Yeshua and his ministry, and had sent him messages of invitation to come to Edessa and cure him of his chronic skin rashes. Yeshua could not accept the invitation at that time, but deputed one of his associates named Thaddeus (Addai in Syriac) with some powders and balms to cure the King. Thaddeus managed to heal the King who sent a special invitation to Yeshua to visit Edessa as his guest in the palace. He had heard about the goings on in Jerusalem, and was saddened by the crucifixion. As nobody had ever come alive from crucifixion and burial, it occurred to the King that he was possibly playing host to a resurrected Yeshua. When Daniel informed him that Yeshua needed rest and recuperation for a few months, the King gladly agreed to be host to this illustrious guest.

King Akbar had his own agenda. He organized periodic healing sessions, when his extended family, including his wives, concubines, children and the palace staff, gathered in the Great Hall of the palace to be healed of their diseases. Yeshua addressed the gathering first, talking about the Kingdom of God, human condition and human behavior with parables as his tool. In the healing session that followed, many were cured of their diseases. After a few months, Daniel got a message from Palestine that there was a crackdown on the Essenes. This was on the basis of a report from the Jewish hierarchy that the followers of Yeshua and the Essenes were planning an armed revolt. The Roman Prefect found that the followers of Yeshua, though they held regular meetings, were neither organized nor capable of armed conflict. But the Essenes were a potential threat. Hence some Essene leaders were arrested. Daniel sought permission to leave immediately with his colleagues. Yeshua agreed, but asked Daniel to request Yosef of Arimathea to stop by at Edessa during his next caravan trip. When Yosef stopped by after a month, Yeshua expressed his interest to go to Taxila, as Palestine was closed for him. Yosef contacted Shakuntala and Guru Shantideva during his next halt in Taxila and conveyed the message. Both of them replied that they would be happy to receive Yeshua. Thus it was arranged that Yeshua would join a future caravan trip to Taxila. Accordingly, Yosef himself came a couple of months later, and escorted Yeshua back to Taxila. This time he traveled as the honored guest of the owner of the caravan. All the people treated him with reverence. He was not allowed to do any work or contribute any service. This was a new experience for him, but in general he enjoyed the journey observing the changing geography as well as sceneries and the changes in climate with altitude and latitude. When they reached Taxila, Yosef insisted that Yeshua should rest for a couple of days in the caravan rest house before going to the University. Meanwhile, Yosef sent messages to the university announcing their arrival. Guru Shantideva personally came to escort Yeshua back to the campus.

EPILOGUE

The scene is Shakuntala's drawing room in Taxila University. The house is decorated for her wedding. Many invitees are present in the drawing room. The guests include Guru Shantideva, several faculty members from the Schools of Languages and Religion and friends of the bride including Physician Sanjeevan. Yeshua enters all dressed up as the bridegroom. He is dressed in a cloak of the type that he was wearing in Palestine but with a turban on his head in Indian style. Yeshua walked up to Shantideva, touched his feet and sought his blessings. The Guru stood up, and putting both hands on Yeshua's head, blessed him and wished all happiness in his wedded life. He made Yeshua to sit on his right side. Shakuntala, the bride, entered next, resplendent in her green sari with golden borders. Her luxuriant hair was pleated and decorated with flowers. A gold necklace, studded with precious stones, surrounded her neck. Both hands were full of gold bangles which she inherited from her mother. Three bridesmaids escorted her into the room. Shakuntala walked straight to Guru Shantideva and touched his feet and sought his blessings. The Guru stood up and put his hands on her head and wished her all happiness. He guided her to the seat on his left. He then stood up and started the proceedings.

Guru Shantideva first made an introductory speech, in which he said that Shakuntala was like a daughter to him from the day she was born. He continued: "After her mother's untimely death, her father brought up the young girl whom I had the privilege of watching closely as she grew up into a beautiful and accomplished woman. She preferred academics to sports and fun, and reached the top in whatever she did. She is a linguist who is proficient in Pali as well as Sanskrit and, more recently in Aramaic. She is an expert on Hinduism and has a good knowledge of Buddhism. Today, if she looks like a princess, don't be surprised, for she is indeed a princess. Her maternal grandfather was cheated of his royal inheritance by a cunning brother, but preferred the life of a farmer rather than fight for his rights. But his academic and intellectual credentials remained impeccable, and Shakuntala seems to have inherited them. I must add here that her intellectual inheritance from her father is equally or even more substantial. Her late father, Acharya Sahadeva was not only a great scholar, but also a pioneer who built up the School of Languages in our University in its present form. She, like her mother, possesses the uncanny ability to choose the right husband. I have unknowingly played a small role in bringing this couple together by sanctioning their joint course in comparative religion, which became very successful. I recently learned that Yeshua is also of the Royal Lineage, as a descendent of King David. However, Yeshua never mentioned this fact during his stay with us. This I attribute to his modest nature. From my personal knowledge I would say that he is a linguist, a scholar on religions and a dedicated preacher as well as healer. He is proficient in several languages ranging from Hebrew and Aramaic to Greek, Pali and Sanskrit. He is a scholar in Judaism, Hinduism and Buddhism. He studied Buddhism in this University and is rated as one of the most outstanding scholars ever to pass out of our School. The course he conducted, along with Shakuntala, on comparative religion was an outstanding success. After achieving such great successes, he left everything and went back to his country to preach about the Kingdom of God and to heal the sick and the broken hearted. This he did without expecting any reward whatsoever. After relentless effort for over three years, the very people whom he was trying to reform almost had him executed. He was saved only because of the timely and clever intervention of a few individuals. It turns out that the loss of the Jews is our gain. We are fortunate to have him back in our University and to be the life partner of my dear daughter, Shakuntala."

Shantideva then asked the bridal couple to stand up facing each other. By way of explanation he said: "Shakuntala wants a Swayamvara style of wedding. This is normally practised by Royal Families who invite princes from other royal families to come for the event in which the bride will choose her groom.

In the present case, the bride has already chosen her bridegroom. The ceremony is only for formalising that selection. When she asked me whether she can opt for Swayamvara, I consented for three reasons. First, she has already made the choice and I consider it her prerogative to choose the form of wedding. Secondly, she can choose a royal practice because she comes from a royal line. Thirdly, it avoids the tricky question of which religious tradition should be followed in the wedding. Last, but not the least, the bridegroom did not object. So I ask Shakuntala to garland the groom of her choice. A bridesmaid brought a tray containing a garland of rose flowers of different colours for which Shakuntala's garden was famous. She picked up the beautiful garland delicately and put it around Yeshua's neck. Guru Shantideva pronounced them man and wife. All the assembled guests clapped their hands.

The marriage ceremony was followed by a sumptuous meal. In deference to the Guru who was an ordained Buddhist monk, the meal was purely vegetarian, but delicious. It was prepared under the careful supervision of the bride, who was a well known culinary expert. She personally planned the menu, selected the vegetables, for which Indus Valley was famous, and purchased selected spices directly from the Southern caravan, which periodically passed through Taxila. She felt satisfied when all the guests ate well and appreciated the dishes. Shakuntala whispered to Yeshua that he should thank the guests before they left. Yeshua said: "Shakuntala and I thank all of you for joining us on the occasion of our wedding. We are deeply grateful to Guru Shantideva for presiding over this function and conducting the wedding. It was the timely action of some friends which saved me from the gallows and brought me here. But they are not here to accept our thanks. However, there is one person here who greatly helped my mission – that is Dr. Sanjeevan whose *ayurvedic* medicines was an integral part of my healing mission. One particular medicine that he had thoughtfully provided is reported to have saved my life. It is in the wards of the School of Medicine that he taught me how to cast out demons. Words are not sufficient to pay my indebtedness to this University which taught me many things. This great centre of learning is the place where one learns new things, where ideas are exchanged and new thoughts are born. Both Shakuntala and I consider ourselves lucky to have had the opportunity to study on this campus."

Shantideva waited until all the guests left, and then beckoned to the bridal couple to come and sit near him. "There are some things I must tell you,

Yeshua", said the aged Guru when both of them were comfortably seated. "First of all, I must express my happiness on your return. From all accounts I have got, your mission was a great success. Your mistake was in underestimating the ruthlessness of the priestly hierarchy. When their existence is threatened, they will go to any length to eliminate the threat. No amount of thanking is sufficient to pay our debts to Yosef of Arimathya and his friends who saved you from the gallows. The University is also happy that you are back. The general opinion among the faculty members is that you must lead a research team on the unity of all religions. I have certified that you are eminently qualified for the job. An important development that has happened very recently is that King Gondophares II has abdicated on account of ill health and his brother has ascended the throne with the name Gondophares III. The new King is very supportive of the University as he recognises that we contribute significantly to Taxila's prosperity and fame. Because of the funds sanctioned by the new King, we are now in a position to create a faculty position for you,"

"Coming back to your mission, it is not totally wasted. It is true that the disciples that you left behind are not very educated. They cannot sustain a movement. This vacuum has been filled by a bright young man whom you have not met. His name is Paul. He is well educated and an expert in Jewish Law. He took upon himself the task of persecuting your followers most of whom believe that you were resurrected from the dead. Their proof is the empty tomb. In my opinion Paul saw a great opportunity in the resurrection story and the virtual absence of any organisation for your followers. He has literally hijacked your movement. The way he did it shows his ingenuity. He says that he had a vision while he was going from Jerusalem to Damascus. He saw a bright light in the sky and fell to the ground, with his eyes blinded by the light. Then he heard a voice from the sky which said: 'Paul, why are you persecuting me?". He asked: "Who are you?" The voice said: "I am Yeshua whom you are persecuting". Paul says he protested that he couldnot see anything. He was then asked to go on to Damascus and meet a believer by the name Ananias. Obviously Paul knew that nobody would believe him unless he made up a story like this. According to his narration, Paul had to be helped by his associates, none of whom heard or saw anything unusual, However, they helped him to reach the city and find Ananias. Naturally Ananias was suspicious; but Paul insisted that it was Yeshua who sent him. The moment Ananias touched him, he regained his vision. Ananias was impressed and became the contact that opened many doors for

Paul to the believers who were meeting together secretly. To further prove his genuineness, Paul went to the synagogue on the Sabbath and preached about Yeshua, the Messiah or Christ. Paul soon recognised that the Greeks were fascinated by the story of Christ. Since he was proficient in Greek language, he could communicate the story of Christ, the Son of God, to the Greek population. He was quick to realise the potential of this approach, because the Greek-speaking population far outnumbered the Hebrew-speaking population. Your followers are already called Christians."

"I am not saying all these things to focus on where you did not succeed, but to learn some lessons from these events. You were a great success in reinterpreting the Jewish scripture by making it broader and by putting the responsibility for ones actions on oneself. But you did not build an organisation to continue your work. Perhaps, the events of the last few days before crucifixion took you by surprise. Secondly, you took on the priestly class head on and left the political masters alone. In every religion or community, the priests play a prominent role. They consider themselves the mediators between God and man. Thus they perform *puja* (prayer) to propitiate the gods, to heal you when you are sick, to ensure success in your endeavours, and to ward off evil from your path. You are dependent on them for these rituals. There is a charge for each ritual, which ensures a good income for the priest. The priests have two benefits from this arrangement: high position in society and monetary income. If you threaten these, they will strike back by eliminating the threat. The other powerful vested interest is the temporal authority. The latter often acts in unison with the former. Your approach of leaving the Government alone did not help because the temporal authority needs the religious hierarchy for survival. This mutual support exists so long as it is beneficial for both. There is conflict when one of the parties poses a threat to the other. This has happened many times in history, but in such conflicts it is the temporal authority that generally wins, and they appoint a new priestly hierarchy. The worst case scenario, as far as the common man is concerned, happens when these two functions are combined. This was the case with Pharaohs of Egypt, under whom the common man paid a heavy price".

"I can explain this with the example of my own religion. Gautama Buddha brought in fresh ideas on the human condition by invoking Dharma. People were happy with his teachings mainly because it proposed that your future depends on your own actions. This relieved them from the heavy burden put on them by the priests for *puja* to propitiate the gods. But it gained wide acceptance quite quickly because of Buddha's royal connections. His mother was one his early followers. She persuaded many other royal families to join the movement. The kings have the power and the monetary resources to withstand the priestly backlash. When Emperor Ashoka joined Buddhism, the movement got a lot of clout, especially financial muscle. Buddha himself realised the need for an organisation and laid the foundation of Sangha. With Buddha and Ashoka gone, human interest came to the forefront in Sangha; and positions of power are sought after. Now you can see the appearance of different streams of Buddhism.

With this background, I would predict great success for Paul. My conclusion is based on three premises. Paul has shrewdly taken off where Yeshua left off after leading a very successful campaign. He bases his religion on the teachings of Yeshua, which got wide acceptance during Yeshua's mission itself. In addition, he has the Jewish scripture as a background document. With his detailed knowledge of the Jewish scriptures, he can build a new theology which shows that the appearance of Yeshua, his death and resurrection as continuation of the Jewish Scriptures. As prophesies given in the Tanaka are very general in nature, he can even find predictions of the birth and life of Yeshua. Secondly, he has recognised that the new religion can be presented to a wider audience including others like the Greek community which has been thirsting for a new theology. It may be recalled that you [Yeshua] had faced the dilemma whether your movement was open to Greeks. You evaded the issue by saying that your primary message was to the circumcised Jews. Paul has already indicated that Greeks need not be circumcised to join the new religion. Thirdly, his movement is focused on Yeshua, the Christ. Since Christ has risen from the dead and ascended into heaven, he cannot come and contradict Paul. The followers of Christ are already being called Christians. The rituals of the new religion are centred around your death and resurrection. At the time of the last supper you had with your disciples, you asked them to continue the practice of Passover Supper in your remembrance, even if you are not present. This is now being made into a ritual. In the new religion, the bread being distributed is presented as the body of Christ and the wine in the chalice as his blood. As a matter of strategy, Paul will definitely give importance to your disciples, who are now called apostles. Apostles are the direct disciples of Yeshua. Paul claims to be an apostle, on account of his direct contact with Christ in his encounter on the road to Damascus. Since he is a well educated man, he will write many epistles which will define the new theology called Christology. If he manages to convert the Greeks who are spread around the rim of the Mediterranean Sea, the new religion will be a force to reckon with. From the history of all such human organisations, we can predict what will happen. So long as the apostles, including Paul, are around their words will be respected. After their time, there will be struggles for power: who is at the top, and who comes next. Since the new leaders are unlikely to be as erudite as Paul, it will be the texts that Paul writes and some records of your teachings that would form the basis of the new religion. This is another example of the importance of education. That is why we welcome you warmly back to Taxila to strengthen our scholastic capital

If Paul's movement grows big, then political authorities will step in. They would want to control the movement and in turn gain legitimacy for their regimes. This leads to corruption which can be directly linked to dispensation of privileges. Corruption appears ubiquitous when those in authority have powers to distribute benefits".

Shantideva once again placed his hands, one each on the heads of the bridal couple, and blessed them. Yeshua thanked him and said: "Thank you, Sir for your words of wisdom. I realise that I cannot go back to my native Palestine. But the fact is that I have come to the best place. I love this place for its verdant green which is the sign of life, the academic freedom and above all for this wonderful woman who is willing to share her life with me. I never aspired for fame, authority or power. What I have got is enough for me, because it makes me happy." So saying, he took Shakuntala's hand and they walked hand in hand behind the departing Shantideva to let him out and start their new life together.

GLOSSARY

1. A	Abraham: Patriarch of Israel
2.	Ashoka: Third Emperor of the Maurya Dynasty.
3.	Adam: The first man created by God, according to Jewish scripture
4.	Acharya: Dean of the University
5.	Acharya Shantideva: Dean of the School of Religion in Taxila University
6.	Acharya Sahadeva: Acharya of the School of Languages in Taxila University
7.	Alexander the Great: Builder of the biggest Empire in the world up to his time
8.	Agni: Hindu God, Lord of fire
9.	Aramaic: Popular language Of Parthia and Palestine; language spoken by Jesus
10.	Ayurveda: System of medicine practiced in India from Vedic times, Medicine based on plants
11.	Arimathea Yosef : A Jewish trader who supported Yeshua
12.	Achaemenid: Dynasty of Persian Kings
13.	*Atman: non-*perishable part of a being

B 14	Bhagwath Gita: Hindu theology, advice of Krishna, reincarnation of Vishnu. Part of Mahabharatha
15	Bar Mitzvah: A ceremony for Jewish males at the age of 12; coming of age of Jewish boys
16	Bindusara: Second King of the Maurya Dynasty.
17	Bhishma: Elder statesman, strategist and military leader in Mahabharata
18	Brahmi: Script of Pali, Inscriptions found on Ashoka Stupas
19	Buddhism: Religion based on Dharma (Buddha's teachings)
20	Baptist, John: Yeshua's cousin and Essene leader who baptised people in River Jordan
21.	Bhishma: Elder statesman and warrior of Hastinapura; He disinherited himself to facilitate his father's second marriage.
22	Brahmanyam: ritual part of *vedas*
23 C	Chanakya: Political strategist of Maurya kings, Economist of Taxila
24	Chandra Gupta: Founder of the Maurya Dynasty
25	Charaka: Physician, Acharya of Taxila School of Medicine
26	Cain and Habel: Sons of Adam
27	Cyrus the Great: Founder of Persian Kingdom
28 D	Dharma: Teachings of Buddha
29	David: Popular King of Israel,
30	Darius I: Third king of Achaemenid dynastyt
31	*Devas*: highest realm of rebirth (Buddhism)
32	Demi-gods: Second highest realm of rebirth (Buddhism)
33 E	Eve: The first woman according to Jewish scripture Euclid:Greek mathematician, known for his work in geometry
34	Eratosthenes: Greek mathematician, first measured the circumference of Earth, invented geography

35	Essenes: A group of Jews who were opposed to Pharisees and Sadducees, as well as Roman rule
36 G	Garden of Eden: Garden planted by God after Creation where Adam was put in charge
37	Great Flood: Flood sent by God to destroy all flora and fauna except two of each species who were saved in Noah's Ark
38	Galilee and Perea: Areas ruled by Herod Antipas at the time of Yeshua
39	Greek: People of Greece; also language spoken by Greeks
40	Gamaliel: Rabbi who was known for his School of Scripture
41	Gondophares: King of Taxila when Yeshua reached there. His successors assumed the same name
42	Goliath: warrior hero of Philistines
43 H	Hanuman: Hindu god, devotee and hatchet man of King Rama
44	Hebrew: Language of Israel, People of Israel
45	Hinduism: religion practiced in India from Vedic times, religion of the Gupta Empire
46	Herod the Great: Ruler of undivided Palestine as a client king of the Romans
47	Herod Antipas: Son of Herod the great. Ruler of Galilee and Perea after Herod died
48	Hastinapura: Kingdom over which Kurukshetra war was fought
49	Hell being: lowest state of birth (Buddhism)
50	Hungry Ghost: Second lowest realm of rebirth (Buddhism)
51 I	Indra: lord of the sky
52 J	Jacob: Abraham's grandson and Patriarch of Israel
53	Joshua: Successor of Moses as leader of Israel

54	Judges: Leaders who rose to leadership of Israel between Joshua and Kings
55	Jerusalem: Capital of Israel
56	Judea: Jewish State with Jerusalem as Capital
57	Jeroboam: Founder of the Northern Kingdom of Israel
58 K	Kapilavastu: Capital of Sakhya Kingdom; Buddha's birthplace
59	Krishna: Hindu God, the divine factor in Mahabharata
60	*Karma*: the algebraic sum of the positive and negative fruits of ones actions
61 L	Lava, Kusha: sons of Rama in Ramayana
62 M	Mahabharatha: Hindu Epic. Story of rivalry between Kauravas and Pandavas
63	Moses: Leader of Israel who led them from Slavery in Egypt to the Promised Land
64	Mount Sinai, Mount Horeb: The mountain where God spoke to Moses.
65	Margala Hills: Hills on the South of Taxila
66	Magadh: Kingdom ruled by Maurya Kings
67	*Moksha:* liberation from rebirth; Atman merges with Paramatman
68 N	Noah's Ark: A huge boat built by Noah as per instructions from YHWH, which floated during the Gr
69	Nazareth: The place where Jesus is believed to have lived his early life
70 P	Pandavas: Five brothers Yudhishtara, Bhima. Arjuna, Nakula and Sahadeva, Heroes of Mahabharata

71	Pharaoh: Emperor of Egypt.
72	Pythagorus: Greek mathematician
73	Pali: Language of Maurya Empire, Language of Ashoka and Buddhism
74	Pontius Pilate: Governor of Judea who ordered crucifixion.
75	Pharisees: The priestly faction of Jews with representation in Sanhedrin
76	Parthian Empire: The empire stretching from Roman Empire in the west to Mauryan Empire in the East in Jesus's time
77	Pataliputhra: capital of Magadh
78	Panini: Grammarian and Acharya of the School of Languages in Taxila University.
79	Potiphar: Chief of Pharaoh's palace guards
80	*Paramatman*: God
81 R	Ramayana: Hindu Epic, Story of King Rama, a reincarnation of Vishnu
82	Rabbi: Jewish teacher
83	Rehoboam: Son of Solomon; King of the Southern Kingdom of Israel
84 S	Sangam: Society of Buddhists
85	Sita: Wife of Rama in Ramayana, Ideal wife
86	Solomon: Wise King of Israel, son of David
87	Shakuntala: Daughter of Acharya Sahadeva, Yeshua's friend
88	Socrates: Greek philosopher
89	Sirkap: Capital of Indo-Parthian Empire; built in Taxila
90	Sadducees: The more influential faction of Jews in Sanhedrin, mainly the scribes
91	Sugriva: estranged brother of Vali, King of Kishkinda

92 T	Ten Commandments: The covenant made by Israel, Ten rules written by god on stone tablets for Israel to follow.
93	Taxila University: ancient University in India, Later a centre for Buddhist studies.
94	Taxila: Seat of ancient university of this name
95	Tanaka: Jewish Scripture
96	Torah:First Five Books of Jewish Scripture, believed to be composed by Moses
97	Tamra Nala: Rivulet flowing through Taxila
98	Takshasila: Old name of Taxila
99 U	Uttar Pada: High Road from Taxila to Pataliputhra
100	*Upanishads*: Theology of *Vedas*
101 V	Veda: Hindu Scripture, Rig Veda, Sama Veda, Yajur Veda, Adharva Veda
102	Varuna: Hindu God, Lord of Water
103	Valerius Gratus: Governor of Judea before Yeshua started his Ministry
104	Valmiki: Sage who composed Ramayana
105	Vyasa: Sage who composed Mahabharatae
106	Vali [Bali]: King of Kishkinda, killed by Rama and replaced by Sugriva
14. W	
15. X	
16. Y	YHWH : God of Israel, pronounced YaHWeH or YAHOWA depending chosen vowels
17. Z	

APPENDIX

Author's Notes

This book represents the author's imagination of how a wholly human Yeshua could have aquired the knowledge and wisdom that was necessary for his ministry in Palestine. The Christian Church believes that Jesus is the Son of God and, therefore, he inherited all this from his Father. But what if his oft-repeated claim to be Son of Man is taken seriously? This book is the story of Yeshua, Son of Man, who educated himself through hard work and toil. Christian believers might find it unacceptable on two counts: [1] Divinity of Jesus is fundamental to their faith and [2] Gospel stories proclaim his divine birth, resurrection and ascension into heaven. However, doubts have been expressed on these two points, some of which are discussed here. This discussion also brings out how the present author was motivated to write this novel.

The Question of Divinity

The divinity of Jesus has been a subject of debate from the early days of Christendom. There were liberal Theological Schools or Seminaries, like the one in Alexandria, where the manhood of Jesus was stressed. Bishop Arius, respected as one of the senior most theologians, taught that Jesus represented the highest level a human being could reach in godliness, without being God. When the Great Council of Nicea started its month long conclave in AD 325, it was generally thought that the Arian line of theology would prevail in the council. Arius argued that the Son was always lower than God, the Father. However this was not acceptable to Emperor Constantine, who was a pagan, but still virtually presided over the conclave. After all, he had convened this assembly of bishops of the Roman Empire in the hope of legitimising his reign through divine endorsement. There were other forces also at work behind the scenes, like personal rivalries among prelates. For example, the popularity of Arius was viewed with suspicion by his superior, Patriarch Alexander of Alexandria, who was egged on by his young colleague Athanasius. The latter was a deacon who was not a delegate to the conclave but came to the Council as an attendant to the Patriarch. The first paragraph of the creed, relating to God the Father, had a smooth sailing as everybody agreed to the wording. It was the second paragraph dealing with Jesus that became contentious. Twenty two bishops actively supported Arius when he argued that the Son was born of the Father, and hence was always lower than the father, Finally, it was the version of Athanasius, which made the Son "con substantial' with the Father, that found favour. The delegates were pressurised into signing the document of faith on the threat of excommunication and exile. In the end only three prelates refused to sign the document - Arius and two supporters from Libya. They were ex-communicated and exiled. Two years later the Emperor regretted his harsh action and reversed the order of exile, and instead exiled Athanasius. Arius died on the way back; but his followers thought that he was poisoned.

In spite of the death of Arius, Arianism refused to die down. In fact, the eastern part the Empire was solidly Arian. The new Holy Sea of Constantinople became the hot bed of dissent to the Nicene Creed. When Theodosius became Emperor in AD 379, he convened a second Great Council to bring about consensus on the Creed. This conclave was held in Constantinople in AD 381. The aim was to adopt a uniform creed for the whole empire. There was one problem. Demophilus, the incumbent Bishop of Constantinople, was an Arian. So the Emperor called the Bishop and offered to confirm him in the post if he gave up Arianism. Demophilus refused, and was ordered to leave. Peter, the Patriarch of Alexandria, wanted to install in Constantinople a bishop who would be subservient to him. His henchmen broke into the Cathedral at night and started consecrating their man as the Bishop. The rival group prevented the completion of this ceremony. The Emperor then ordered that only a cleric who would swear allegiance to the Nicene Creed could become the bishop of Constantinople. Since no one qualified from the Patriarchate, the Emperor chose Gregory Nazianzus as bishop. The Council started with Patriarch Meletius of Antioch as President. But he died soon after and therefore the Emperor offered the Chair to Gregory, who was meanwhile consecrated as Bishop of Constantinople. Facing strong opposition to his chairmanship, Gregory resigned. The Great Council now continued its deliberations under the chairmanship of Nestamus, an unbaptised civil official. The council adopted a canon banning all forms of Arianism from the Church. It also completed the creed by adding two more paragraphs: one about the Holy Spirit and the other about the Holy Catholic Church. Many delegations objected to the Chairmanship of a civil official and refused to accept the decisions of the Council. If the Emperor thought that the matter would end there, he was mistaken.

Later, when Nestorius became Archbishop of Constantinople in AD 428, he found that two interpretations of Christology were prevalent in the Patriarchate. One group argued that Jesus was fully man while on earth, while the other group believed that he was always fully God. Nestorius came up with what he thought was a compromise formula. He put forward the proposal that Jesus had two natures. When he lived on earth, he was fully man, while in heaven, he was fully God. One consequence of this was that Mary, mother of the human Jesus, could not be venerated as Mother of God. The Pope had already done this veneration. Thus when Nestorius succeeded in persuading Emperor Theodosius II to convene a third Ecumenical Council at Ephesus in AD 431, the Nestorian proposal was vehemently opposed not only by Rome, but also by the more orthodox of oriental Patriarchates like Antioch and Alexandria. In the end, the Great Council of Ephesus, denounced the Nestorian thesis as heresy, and Nestorius was removed from his post and exiled. However, Nestorius remained a Saint of the Eastern Church, which never accepted the Nicene Creed in the first place. It may be recalled that the three Great Councils were called into session by the Roman Emperor and only churches in the Roam Empire were represented. As the controversy did not die down, another Ecumenical Council was convened by a later Emperor Marcia. This fourth Council held in AD 451 at Chalcedon included the Church of the East. It decided that Jesus indeed had two natures: Godhead and Manhood. As God he was con-substantial with God the Father; as man he was con-substantial with human beings. This was accepted by the Roman

Catholic Church and the Church of the East. But it was rejected by the Oriental Orthodox Churches of Egypt. Syria, Armenia, Ethiopia etc. The former group came to be known as Bi-physites, while the latter were called Monophysites. Because of this difference, this event came to be known as East-West schism. Though there were several synods held after that, none of them is accepted as Ecumenical Council by a majority of the Churches. No further developments relevant to our subject happened in the Middle Ages, except the consolidation of the Roman Catholic Church in Europe and their efforts to establish themselves in the East by questionable methods, such as the schism in the Church of the East (1552) and the infamous Synod of Diamper (1599). Meanwhile, the Church of the East became weak on account of attacks by the Ottoman Empire. This period also saw the reformation, which resulted in the formation of the Protestant Churches in the sixteenth century

The Age of Enlightenment, which was a period of a couple centuries centred around 1800 AD, was dominated by intellectuals like philosophers. scientists, writers and statesmen. Enlightenment brought in the approach of questioning everything and looking for evidence, rather than going by traditions, practices and dogmas. The Copernican-Galilean model of the universe brought about a systematic understanding of the movements of stars and planets. Newton's Laws made it possible to predict movements of objects, big and small. Darwin's theory of evolution pioneered the way for understanding how the various living specie developed. Thomas Huxley, who supported and propagated Darwin's theory, coined the word 'agnostic', which he proudly displayed as his religion. Agnostics placed themselves between atheists and believers, because they were not sure that God existed or not. It was only natural for the leaders of the Age of Enlightenment to question the divinity of Jesus. American Revolution and the Declaration of Independence are considered the products of the Age of Enlightenment. Thomas Jefferson, the fourth President of the United States of America, made a 'Jefferson Bible' by removing all references to the divinity of Jesus from the gospels. However, these were efforts of intellectuals, but the common man was happy with a Divine Jesus.

The next occasion when this question of divinity came up internationally was when the Soviet Cosmonaut Yuri Gagarin went to outer space in 1961 as the first human being to orbit the earth. Newspapers the world over reported his statement that he found no God up there. In response to that, Bishop Robinson of Woolwich wrote a book entitled: "Honest to God". The essence of that book was that God may not necessarily be found "up there". He argued that the common belief that God resides up in the sky needs revision. He quoted Paul Tillich, Professor of Theology in Harvard University, who had earlier published a book; "Shaking the Foundation", in which he suggested that we should look for God deep within us. Bishop Robinson's book was received with enthusiasm by the liberals, but denounced by the orthodox, No active follow up of these ideas has emerged ever since, In other words, the general public appeared content with a God up there, who can be propitiated by offerings in cash or kind, through the mediation of priests and faith healers. The present author is of the view that this is not what Jesus taught,

The purpose of this book is not to argue for or against the question of divinity, but to explore the possibility that Jesus was fully human. The author is a great admirer of Jesus and a person striving to live by his genuine teachings and to follow his example. If Jesus was not God, the question arises as to how he acquired so much knowledge, great wisdom and a deep insight into human behaviour, at a time when there was no printed literature, very few written documents and restricted access to even those documents. This is where we can let our imagination take wings, charting a course that Jesus could have taken to achieve what he did in his life. To distinguish this human individual from Jesus the Christ, we call him Yeshua, Son of Man. The reader is invited to join in this exciting journey,

The Son of Man is the term that Jesus used for himself. It is used a total of eighty one times in the four gospels put together. In calling himself Son of Man, Jesus was obviously stressing his human origin. On the other hand, the Christian Church adopted the story of Immaculate Conception to account for his divine origin. This raises several questions. The fertilisation of a female egg by the sperm of a male of the same species is the method of procreation in the Animal Kingdom. Immaculate Conception assumes that God, who is the creator and preserver of the universe with its millions of galaxies spread over billions of light years, belongs to the human species. This is a far-fetched assumption that has no basis. We live in an era when astronomers have probed most of the universe with rockets and space vehicles carrying powerful telescopes. An example is the Kepler probe, which has produced evidences of earth-like planets in some far away galaxies. Therefore, it is difficult to limit God to the human species. In this context, a human Jesus becomes very relevant. All human beings have the potential to grow to be like

God in character and behaviour. Perhaps that is what Jesus meant when he called himself Son of man

If Jesus was Son of Man, our story must explain how he acquired all his knowledge and wisdom. If Jesus was God, he could be born with all the knowledge of God. If he was man, he had to gain it through education. The missing years in the life of Jesus between the ages of twelve and thirty may hold the key to this. In this book, it is suggested that the journey of Yeshua, in his quest of knowledge, took him to Taxila University and to his encounter with Buddhism and Hinduism. The result was Yeshua, Son of Man, in whom we find the synthesis of the best of all religions of that period in history.

Gospel Accounts

Gospels do not uniformly discuss the divine birth, resurrection and ascension of Jesus. For example, the Gospel according to St. Mark does not mention any immaculate conception or divine birth with angels singing halleluiah. Further, the shorter version of Mark's gospel does not mention either the resurrection or the ascension. The author of this book became aware of this in his student days when he noticed that the family bible in his mother tongue [Malayalam] showed within brackets the portion after verse 8 of Chapter 16. The brackets meant that the text within them [after verse 8] was added later. If that is so, the resurrection, the great commission and ascension were not in the original text. Since the gospels in the Malayalam version were translated from old Syriac texts, they could be taken as more authentic than the English translations. Critical scholars of the gospels point out that the additions found in the longer version must have been added much later. For example, according to James Tabor, important church fathers like Clement of Alexandria and Origen, both of whom lived in the third century AD, did not know about the longer version. Bishop Eusebius, the compiler of the canon of New Testament books which was adopted by the Nicene Council, has testified that none of the Greek versions of Mark's gospel had the long ending. In the original version, Chapter 16 started with the visit of the three women – Mary Magdalene, Mary mother of James and Salome to the tomb before dawn on the day after Sabbath, and found the heavy stone door rolled away. There was a white-clad young man [not an angel] sitting inside who told them not to look for Jesus in the sepulchre as he had risen and will go to Galilee. The women were so scared that they did not tell anybody about this event. There ended the narration.

It would be interesting to pursue the question: when was the additional text added to the gospel? It is now generally accepted that St. Mark's gospel was the first to be written, most probably in AD fifties. The other three gospels are dated to 80s or 90s. What happened in between these dates to inspire the addition of divine birth, resurrection and ascension? We notice that the epistles of Paul were written from early fifties to his death in the sixties. In his epistles, Paul invokes the blood of Jesus to wash away the believers' sins [Epistle to Ephesians], and institutes the ritual of *eucharist*, the partaking of the body and blood of Jesus [I Cor. 11:23-25]. This was a necessity for Paul to defend himself, as he had never personally known Jesus, was an apostle by self-certification and had fallen out with Jewish Christians on his stand against the Law in discarding the need for circumcision. It was a brilliant move because it was accepted by the Greek Christians, who constituted the church outside of Palestine. It would not be surprising if Paul's views influenced the writers of the later gospels. After all, these gospels were written and propagated in Greek. It can be safely concluded that divinity, resurrection and ascension of Jesus continue to be in doubt.

Printed in the United States
By Bookmasters